HOW TO MANAGE A CITY

A Practitioner's Perspective

Ronald L. Olson

BookLocker

Trenton, Georgia

Print ISBN: 978-1-64719-924-1
Ebook ISBN: 978-1-64719-925-8

Published by BookLocker.com, Inc., Trenton, Georgia.

Printed on acid-free paper.

BookLocker.com, Inc.
2022

First Edition

Library of Congress Cataloguing in Publication Data
Olson, Ronald L.
How to Manage a City: A Practitioner's Perspective by Ronald L. Olson
Library of Congress Control Number: 2021923070

DISCLAIMER

This book is about the author's personal experiences with and opinions about managing cities under the Council/Manager plan. The author acknowledges that others may have differing opinions and contrary experience.

The author and publisher are providing this book and its contents on an "as is" basis and make no representations or warranties of any kind with respect to this book or its contents. The author and publisher disclaim all such representations and warranties, including for example warranties of merchantability and technical advice for a particular purpose. In addition, the author and publisher do not represent or warrant that the information accessible via this book is accurate, complete or current.

Any statements made about products and services have not been evaluated by the U.S. government. Please consult with your own legal, accounting, medical, technical, or other licensed professional regarding the suggestions and recommendations made in this book.

Except as specifically stated in this book, neither the author or publisher, nor any authors, contributors, or other representatives will be liable for damages arising out of or in connection with the use of this book. This is a comprehensive limitation of liability that applies to all damages of any kind, including (without limitation) compensatory; direct, indirect or consequential damages; loss of data, income or profit; loss of or damage to property and claims of third parties.

You understand that this book is not intended as a substitute for consultation with a licensed medical, legal, technical, accounting, or other professional. Before you begin any change to your management techniques or lifestyle in any way, you will consult a licensed professional to ensure that you are doing what's best for your situation.

Ronald L. Olson

This book provides content related to the author's experience regarding city management and local government political topics. As such, use of this book implies your acceptance of this disclaimer.

Table of Contents

Introduction

The Council-Manager plan of city government and the city management profession were born out of the good government movement in the United States during the early part of the 20th century. The intent of that movement was to take corruption out of city government and replace it with ethical performance, efficiency and fairness. City Managers continue to play a key role in accomplishing those goals even today. This book chronicles my career in the profession, what I learned and the management style I developed. It will provide insights and discussion points for both students and practitioners; for others it will provide a window into the operations of the cities in which they live.

Before I finished my bachelor's degree, I served an enlistment in the US Army, primarily stationed at Fort Lewis, WA. During that time, I took several college courses to further my education. My long-term goal was to finish my university training when my term of military service was completed. In one of the courses, the professor suggested that I consider a career in Public Administration as it was an up-and-coming discipline that was gaining a lot of popularity. I rejected the suggestion rather quickly because all my previous thinking had focused on Business Administration in the private sector. However, several years later, when I was out of the Army and finishing my bachelor's degree, I reconsidered. After a lot of soul-searching, I realized that just earning a living wasn't going to be fulfilling for me. I needed to feel like I was contributing to a bigger cause and performing an important service. So, I reconsidered Public Administration.

After completing a bachelor's degree, I entered the Master of Public Administration program at Brigham Young University. Inside of Public Administration, there are many areas of specialty; I had no clue which to choose. This specific graduate program was a two-year, terminal degree program with a required internship between the first and second year. The first year was comprised of general classes and the second year allowed for more specialization. Quite by accident, I

1

was fortunate to get an internship in my hometown of West Jordan, Utah. During that internship I worked in most of the functional areas of city service. I collected garbage, worked with the water and sewer crews, paved streets, went on patrol with the police, did office work and utility billing, attended City Council meetings and much more. By the time the summer had passed, I was hooked on city management and spent my second year of graduate work specializing in that area.

When I finished working on my Master of Public Administration degree, I was tired of the classroom and of being a student. I was anxious to go to work and get on with life. Later however, after the pain of class work and strain of financial sacrifice for education had been dimmed, I began to consider going back to school for a doctorate in Public Administration. While in this state of mind, I met a person with a PhD who suggested that I was in the perfect position as a practitioner to study and test various management theories and techniques. He said that, in many ways, it was better than being an academic who had the blessing of learning, but not implementing management theory. I have always been grateful for that advice and from that point on, I considered my city my laboratory. I am a pragmatic city management practitioner…. and proud of it. I looked for what worked. I picked up ideas from books, seminars, conferences, and from my City Manager colleagues. I tested the ideas. I modified them. I innovated. I kept what worked and I discarded what didn't. Over time, I developed a rather personalized and unique style of management that worked very well for me. I'm not saying it was the best style for everyone, or better than anyone else's style. I'm just saying that it worked very well for me and benefited the cities I served.

Several years ago, when I was City Manager in Corpus Christi, Texas, I met with a small group of pastors from various Christian denominations who were interested in the welfare of the city. Because of their keen interest in the issues of the city and how those issues affected the lives of people they served, they met with me to add their faith to the work that I was doing. We met regularly and talked about the challenges, the real issues behind the news reports, the sensitivity of personal relationships in the organization, and the hard decisions that had to be made to fix what was commonly thought of as a dysfunctional city. They were a good sounding board for me, and I shared many of my strategies and plans to accomplish my work with them. Over time, the conditions in the city organization began to improve, relationships between people began to improve, and the confidence of the residents toward their city government began to improve. I appreciated their counsel and I believe they began to appreciate the complexities and difficulties of managing that city. Further, they expressed appreciation for the techniques and processes I used to do my work. After several years of this pattern, they suggested that I write a book that might help others who are engaged in leading and managing cities. I have thought much about that suggestion; in a way, it has haunted me. I decided to take the suggestion and write a book about my management techniques.

As I have considered it, I have realized that there are many dedicated people in my profession. Many of them have attended graduate school and studied public administration, but, like me, they best learn the craft of city management, not from books or the classroom, but from real life experience. Every City Manager I know has his own management style, own management philosophy and own view of the systems required to run a complex municipal organization. With full respect and admiration for my colleagues, I am hopeful that I can describe my management style in a way that will spark new ideas for some of them, especially the less experienced ones. Hopefully, they too will be able to test their new ideas and innovate as they search for their own best management style.

For those who are not engaged in managing cities, perhaps they can gain a greater appreciation for how important cities are and how they work. For still others who manage non-profit organizations, other local governments, or even private sector organizations, perhaps some of the techniques and principles I intend to express in this book may find a place in their management styles as well.

As for myself, I have retired from the profession that I have loved and committed more than four decades of my life to. Though retired, I still often dream of managing the city. As I practice this new retirement phase of life, hopefully, this book will help me clear my mind by chronicling the things I have learned and practiced.

Why is this book important? The basic answer to that question is because cities are important. They make a big difference in our lives. Most people in the United States live in an incorporated city. For the portion of the population that does not live within the city limits, they too rely on the nearby city for shopping, employment, social life and occasionally, even some municipal services. From those cities, we receive reliable, clean water; our garbage is regularly collected and disposed of; there are parks for our children to play in; storm water is managed to keep flooding away from our homes; building codes are enforced for our safety; zoning and nuisance codes are enforced to ensure we are safe and to maintain our private property values; streets are built and maintained for us to drive our cars and to promote freedom of movement and mobility; and our public safety is further provided for in the form of police, fire and emergency medical service. It is not insignificant that the elected and appointed people who make decisions about these services are our neighbors and easily accessible to hear our concerns. Those officials are as concerned as we are about the quality of service being provided because they receive that service, too. They are concerned about the taxes and fees needed to pay for those services, and they are concerned about finding the balance required to make our communities both livable and affordable. This is democracy…right at our doorsteps. It is self-government closest to the people. Even though many of the services cities provide are taken completely for granted, they touch us every single day of our lives. The cities we live in absolutely make a daily difference in the quality of our lives.

This book is important because it explains how to manage Cities at peak efficiency, how to create management systems and processes that allow decision-makers to determine what is most important and where to prioritize the use of scarce resources. It explains how to ask the right questions, get the right answers, and make good decisions. It explains how to communicate both successes and challenges in an honest, transparent way. It explains how to transform a financially challenged, mismanaged and untrusted city into a high performance, respected, benchmark organization.

Why am I qualified to write this book? For more than 40 years, I have been a public servant. I have served six cities and one county in communities ranging from 6,000 population to over 400,000. I have been a Finance Director, Deputy City Manager, County Manager and City Manager. My experience has not been one year of experience, multiplied 40 times but rather, 40 diverse and unique years of, sometimes, bone-grinding experience.

I was a pragmatic practitioner, not an academic, and I continued to be a learner of techniques and practices that worked throughout my career. I asked questions and tried to find the principles behind successful management actions. I shaved the fluff off theory and moved to the core of practical application. I would always go for what works. Some people try to build job security by complicating things and wrapping process and function in mystery. I, on the other hand, spent a working lifetime trying to simplify complicated things and make them understandable. My measuring stick was always whether an eighth grader could understand an issue. If an eighth grader could understand it, we had simplified it enough.

When I was a graduate student at Brigham Young University, one of my professors, who had himself been a successful City Manager, told me that there were two ways to become a good City Manager: first, leave school and go to work for a proven, successful City Manager who can show you how to do it right; second, leave school and go to work for an inexperienced City Manager where you can learn from their mistakes. Either course can ultimately get you to the same place – being a successful City Manager. More by happenstance than anything else, I followed the second course. Some of the most important lessons I have learned throughout my career have been from the school of hard knocks. Mistakes can be some of our most important teachers when we learn from them and don't magnify our errors. Experimentation and risk-taking are critical to learning. I hope that my experience as expressed in this book can shortcut the learning process for others and save them from the same hard knocks I experienced.

Even the best managed, smoothest operating cities will have plenty of challenges. I have learned to love and appreciate working in challenging cities because my biggest learning experiences have come from my most challenging situations. In fact, I came to the point that I would only consider working in cities that needed to be fixed because the biggest improvements can be made in those cities by applying basic principles of good management. I considered fixing broken cities to be my specialty.

I believe that all this experience qualifies me to write this book, chronicle my knowledge, and share it with others for their profit and learning. All of which, I sincerely hope, will contribute to making our cities better places in which to live.

THE
CITY

The City

Background

I was recently talking to my barber who was in Dublin, Ireland, when that city was celebrating its 1,000th anniversary. Being an American, it is hard for me to grasp the idea that a city could be over 1,000 years old, but many cities are ancient. Arguably, Damascus, Syria for example is one of the oldest cities; it has been continuously inhabited since the second millennium BC and may have been established as early as 10,000 BC. Other cities from around the globe and from all continents have been established or inhabited for thousands of years. A quick internet search will provide one with an idea of how old ancient cities really are and where the oldest ones are located. I'm not trying to be a historian, an archaeologist, or an anthropologist. There are people who know much more about this subject than I do. My point is simple: Cities have been around for a long time. Many of them predate the states or nations in which they are currently located. Many cities predate any accurate historical record, forcing us to speculate on their age, origin and purpose.

What are cities and where did they come from?

People who know about these things theorize that cities came into existence when human beings began to successfully practice agriculture. When people no longer had to worry every day about their next meal, they could specialize in crafts and trades in addition to hunting and gathering. Cities became the gathering places where people could live close to their work, where they could interact with people to trade their goods. Anciently, cities were places where people and resources came together; they were the economic engines that drove their society. They still are today.

Over time, each city develops its own unique characteristics. Some cities specialize in certain kinds of commerce. Other cities focus on their culture, their climate or their livability. Still others are plain and simply known for their hometown atmosphere. No matter their uniqueness, they are all places where people gather, live and trade.

Cities come in all sizes. Some are very large. New York City, for example, has a population more than 8.5 million. Other cities are villages with populations in the hundreds. When thinking about cities, it is common for people to envision the large cities with skyscrapers and very large populations. That is not the reality for most cities in America. Most American cities are relatively small, with populations much less than 20,000. They are governed locally; they are managed locally.

Much of the ancient history of cities is speculative; so really, it is more interesting than practical. From this pragmatic practitioner's point of view, what matters is, not the history and origin of cities, but the fact that they exist. We live in them. They need to be managed well for everyone's benefit.

What is the Federal System of government?

To better understand today's American cities, one must understand the environment in which they exist. That environment is called the Federal System of government. What I mean by "federal system" is a system of layers of government. The United States Constitution recognizes two layers of government, the government of the United States and the governments of the various States. Sometimes we refer to the government of the United States as the Federal Government. That is not the same as the "federal system" of government and it can be confusing. Sometimes we refer to the government of the United States as the National Government, sometimes just The Government. The fact that there are two layers, the national government and the state government, makes it a federal system.

Inside of the state governments, there are also layers, often referred to as political subdivisions of the state. For example, the states are typically divided into counties. The counties receive their authority and limitations from the state constitution and state laws. Within the counties, but separate from them, are cities. Cities are incorporated jurisdictions that also receive their authority and limitations from the state constitution and state laws. Some, but not all, states have variations that allow cities to become "home rule" cities by adopting a Charter, which gives them a level of independence from state law. Some states, but not all, have unincorporated jurisdictions like cities called townships, which are intended to serve a more rural population and have fewer powers than cities. Similarly, school districts are political subdivisions of the state as are other special purpose districts of various kinds. Each of these levels of government have elected officials who set policy and make decisions for their unit of government, including taxation and the raising of revenue to operate that government. Taken all together, they make up the Federal System of government.

Why are cities thought of as being the government closest to the people?

Cities are often thought of as being lowest in the pecking order of the federal system, ranking below the Federal Government, State Government, and County Government. Another way of looking at it is, City Government is that which is closest to the people, the place where democracy is administered right where we live, right at our doorstep. Cities provide basic services which touch where and how we live every single day: providing reliable and clean water; collecting and disposing of our garbage; building and maintaining parks; installing and managing storm water facilities to keep flooding away from our homes; enforcing building codes for our safety; providing zoning and nuisance codes to ensure we are safe and to maintain our private property values; constructing and maintaining streets and sidewalks to promote freedom of movement and mobility; improving public health through health department programing; and providing for our public safety through police, fire, emergency medical service and disaster response.

Of significant importance is the fact that our cities are governed by the people who live in them. Mayors and Council Members are elected by their neighbors to make decisions about the services to be provided along with the taxation needed to pay for those services. It is not some unknown bureaucrat or political operator in a place far, far away imposing taxes and requirements on the people of our city. It is our neighbors; people who are as invested in the place in which we live as we are; and people who dislike taxation as much as we do. It is people we vote for and, therefore, people we can trust. It is people we can sit down with and talk with face to face. The decisions made by these select, elected representatives will more directly affect our quality of life than any other level of government. Note: If you believe that what I have just described does not exist in your city, it is your own fault and only you can fix it. Get informed. Get involved. Go vote. Every voice in city government makes a difference.

How does a City work?

Cities are part of the federal system of government, and they are at the bottom of the political ladder. While Cities are subject to being regulated by the State, and somewhat by the National, governments, this ranking also places them as the unit of government easiest to access by the governed. To effectively access city government, people must know how it works. So, the next logical question is this: How does a city work?

That is not a simple question to answer because cities can be structured in many ways. Some cities are governed by City Councils, others by Commissions, and still others by Boards of Aldermen. Most cities have either a Strong Mayor or a Weak Mayor (referring to the form of government, not the personality of the Mayor). Some have no Mayor at all but do have Chairpersons of the elected body. Some cities have City Managers while others may have City Administrators or City Supervisors and still others may have none. I will attempt to explain this in a little more detail and with a little more clarity.

A traditional Commission form of government is one in which each elected official oversees an area of responsibility in the city. For example, one elected official might be the Commissioner of Public Safety and oversee the police and fire departments. Another might be the Commissioner of Streets and oversee the street department. Another might be the Commissioner of Utilities and oversee the water and sewer departments. A traditional Commission does not have a Mayor but, rather, a chairperson. The position of Chair is generally selected by the Commission itself, and not by a public election. The responsibilities of serving as Chair are often rotated between commissioners.

A Weak-Mayor city government is one in which the Mayor chairs the City Council, has no executive authority beyond membership on the Council, and generally does not vote.

A Strong-Mayor city government is one in which the Mayor has executive authority to appoint and remove personnel, exercise a veto, has power independent of the Council.

In a Council-Mayor form of government, the Mayor is the Chief Executive Officer of the city and is responsible for both chairing the Council and overseeing the operations of the city. The department heads are responsible to the Mayor. This form of government is most often a strong Mayor format. A variation of the Council-Mayor form is when the Mayor is required to have a professional City Administrator (like a Chief of Staff or a Chief Operating Officer) who reports to the Mayor and is responsible to the Mayor for the daily operations of the city. In this form of government, department heads report to the Mayor through the City Administrator.

In a Council-Manager form of government, the City Manager is the Chief Executive Officer of the city and is responsible to the City Council (of which the Mayor is a part) for the operations of the City. This form of government is almost always a weak Mayor format. The department heads are responsible to the City Manager. In this form of government, the Mayor is the chair and spokesperson for the City Council and is the Chief Ceremonial Officer of the city. This form of government is like the business model where a CEO runs a company under the policy guidance of a Board of Directors. Although it is important to understand the various forms that a city government may function under, this book is focused on the Council-Manager system.

Under either the Council-Mayor or the Council-Manager forms of government, City Councils can be elected either at-large or by geographically defined districts (wards, precincts, etc.) or combinations thereof.

The responsibilities of all the positions mentioned above are very important to the efficient operation of cities. Without good policy, a City Manager will find it difficult to succeed. Without good management, the City Council will find it difficult to be successful. Because we have such open government, some people mistakenly believe that simply anyone can be successful in leading and managing a government jurisdiction. That perception is not accurate. In today's world, things are increasingly complex. Even since I was a teenager in the 1960's things have become more complicated, and the 60's were not exactly an easy time. For example, back then, I could service my own car. I could change the oil, replace spark plugs and set the timing. Today, not so much. Back then, young people experimented with alcohol; today they experiment with drugs. Back then, a 10-key adding machine was quite the technology; today there is more computing power in our cell phones than what they used to put a man on the moon. Back then, there was people drama; today people drama is multiplied exponentially by social media. Everything is more complex and complicated today, including government.

Let me give you a few examples from city government. Policing, for example, is more complex because of increasingly complex social challenges in our society such as drugs, domestic relationships, and political correctness. Policing is made even more complicated by our complex legal system, making it difficult to recruit candidates into law enforcement because of the social and legal complexities that make the personal liabilities so risky. Water and wastewater treatment are controlled by the Clean Water Act, making it very scientific and complex. Open Meetings Laws and Freedom of Information requirements place heavy administrative requirements on local governments. Building Codes are extensive and constantly changing. I could go on and on. I'm not saying that these things are bad. In fact, they are all generally good for our society. They do make local government more complicated and more costly. Combine that with the fact that, for every issue, there seems to be some that want more of it and some that want less. These competing values and priorities make conflict in local government a constant reality as well.

My observation is that people are seeking simple solutions to local government problems that simply don't exist. The issues are complex and so are the solutions. This can be very frustrating.

What are the major differences between the National, State and Local Governments?

As previously mentioned, cities are governments and fit within the federal system of government. In 1869, John Forrest Dillon, a judge on the Iowa Supreme Court, rendered an opinion that Municipal Corporations were entirely subject to the authority of their state; that they are institutions created by the state and, therefore, can be amended or eliminated at the will of the state. This is Dillon's Rule; it says that cities have only those powers granted to them by the state. Although challenged, it has been relied upon in many US Supreme Court rulings and still stands today. Cities are creatures of the states in which they are located, meaning they derive their power and authority from the state government and are subject to the limitations that the state legislature or the state constitution places upon them. As creatures of the state, cities are generally classified into one of two categories: General Law cities or Home Rule cities. General Law cities derive their power from the statutes of the state and have only those powers enumerated in the law. If the law is silent on a particular aspect of city government, cities cannot act in that area. A second approach to city government is Home Rule. Some states allow cities to adopt a unique charter, rather than relying solely upon the general laws of the state, to govern themselves. In those municipalities and under the authority of the state, cities adopt, through an election process, a Home Rule Charter. The Charter performs like a constitution for that specific city and may vary from the general state law governing other cities in that state. Even then, many of the state laws governing cities may still apply to a Home Rule City. It can be confusing and must be interpreted on a case-by-case basis.

Politically, cities differ from national, state and county government in that most cities (except the very largest ones) are non-partisan, meaning that a person does not need to be affiliated with a political party to run for public office. That is not to say that individual municipal elected officials are not affiliated with a political party. In most cities, party politics is usually not involved in the campaign process nor are candidates identified by their party affiliation in the election. City Councils typically do not divide themselves into caucuses and do not vote along party lines as a standard practice.

Unlike the national government, state, county, and city governments are required to balance their budgets. Therefore, elected city leaders are continuously making very difficult choices about service priorities versus the city's ability to pay. There is never enough money to do all that is needed or wanted. City Councils and Staff are under constant pressure from their constituency, who seem to have the mistaken notion that they should get everything they want from city government yet not have to pay any more for it. It is impossible to count the number of times I have heard citizens say something like, if you can do A (something they don't particularly want), then you can also do B (something they do want). The truth is, in city government, there is a finite amount of money. If you spend it on A, you cannot spend it on B. The real issue becomes one of setting priorities. Sometimes constituent expectations can be unrealistic. I recall one time that a resident appeared before one of my City Councils and wanted emergency medical services extended to her pets. She said something like this: If you can spend money for a high-priced consultant to study road conditions, you can also spend money to provide emergency medical services to our pets.

Unlike the national government, cities borrow money for major capital projects such as roads or buildings but do not borrow money for operating expenses (with the rare but possible exception of Tax Anticipation Notes, which is only stop-gap borrowing until property taxes are received within that same fiscal year.) Funding is a difficult and thankless responsibility. Under the US Constitution, only the national government can print and coin money. Cities only sometimes wish they could.

Because cities are at the beginning of the political ladder, it is relatively easy and routine for the national and state governments to establish regulations that require municipal compliance. A few quick examples include water and air quality, provision of public information, investment standards, various work rules and safety requirements, and accommodation for disabilities. There are many more. Worthy as these regulations may be, the cost of implementation is primarily borne by the city and not the higher government that created them. Occasionally, the higher governments will even exempt themselves from the very regulation that they pass on to cities. For example, Congress has exempted itself from parts or all of the Freedom of Information Act, various labor and employment regulations, and OSHA standards. For cities, this type of regulation is referred to as an "unfunded mandate." From my experience, I estimate that most of the cost of city government is a result of unfunded mandates.

To the casual observer these differences between national, state and local governments may seem minor, but they are significant. My theory is that many people get frustrated with the National Government because of partisan politics, sharp differences about both social and financial policy and then they transfer that frustration to city government. Because city government is closest to the people and most easily accessible, it very often takes the brunt of that frustration in a manner and at a level that it does not deserve.

What are City Managers and what do they do?

I cannot begin to estimate the number of times someone has asked me what I do for a living and then after I respond, they ask, what is a City Manager? Often, they will immediately follow that question with another: Is that the same as a City Planner or is it an Assistant to the Mayor? Each time that happens, I am surprised at how uninformed people are about how cities work. No, a City Manager is not the same as a City Planner. No, it is not an Assistant to the Mayor.

A City Manager is the Chief Executive Officer of the municipal corporation and is responsible to the governing body for the operational performance of the entire city.

The next question usually asked is this: What does a City Manager do? For a long time, I struggled to give a concise answer to that question. Typically, I would say, manage the operations of the city or carry out the policies of the City Council. These answers are, of course, correct but they are also incomplete.

Most City Charters (State laws or city ordinances) have a chapter outlining the duties of the City Manager. It is somewhat of a job description. The Charter basically outlines <u>what</u> must be done but it doesn't say anything about <u>how</u> it should be done. Charters do not give the necessary clarity for a full understanding of what it takes for someone to be good at the craft of city management. In addition to any language in a Charter, Law, Ordinance or job description, my experience teaches me that there are four primary duties that one must master to be good at city management. They are as follows:

1. Leadership,
2. Advising the City Council,
3. Managing City Operations, and
4. Engaging people.

The balance of this book will elaborate on each of these four duties and describe, in very practical ways, how each of them function.

LEADING

a City

Leadership

The City Manager's First Duty

My first day on the job as an intern was an eye opener. Arrangements had been made for me to meet with the City Manager in front of City Hall to begin my first day. I was excited for the experience to begin so I arrived at 7:00 am, an hour early, and sat in my car, waiting for my meeting. As I sat there two men in city-marked pickups pulled into opposite sides of the small parking lot. As it turned out, one was the City Manager and the other was the "Work Director." They got out of their vehicles, walked toward each other and stopped right in front of my car. They didn't notice I was there. They were both talking in loud voices, with animated arm movements. They were having what seemed to be completely different conversations, on different topics. They were both talking at the same time, neither of them apparently listening to the other. Their meeting lasted for only a few short minutes, then, quickly as it had begun, it ended. Both men stopped talking, quickly turned toward their vehicles and left. I sat wondering what had just occurred and how successful my summer internship would be.

Over the years, I have worked for and with leaders of all types and styles. Each was unique; some were dominant, others were more passive, most were effective, but others not so much. Some were good at adjusting their style to meet the requirements of the circumstances; others had just one dominant style. I have concluded that there is no one style that is best for everyone or for every situation. Each leader must find a style that fits her individual personality and temperament.

That puts me in mind of an experience I had as a teenager: When I was in high school, I had a part-time job in a small neighborhood market. One of my responsibilities was to look after the produce, including trimming and bagging lettuce from a crate of about two dozen heads. One day, the owner of the market approached me and was critical of the way I was bagging lettuce. After some discussion, we decided a contest was in order to determine which method was best, his or mine. His style was more refined than mine. He carefully trimmed the heads of lettuce; he meticulously opened a plastic bags, then scrupulously rolled the plastic bag around each head. I, on the other hand, wielded the trimming knife like a machete, grabbed the plastic bag and gave it a sharp flick, then jammed the lettuce into the bag. At the end of the contest, both cases of bagged lettuce looked exactly the same but I had beaten him by a few seconds of time. I am certain that, if he had used my technique, it would have felt clumsy and would have taken him much longer to finish the task. Same for me if I had tried to do it his way. My conclusion was that each person must learn to "bag lettuce" in her own way. So, it is with leadership. Each person desiring to be a leader must find the common principles and practices which, when applied in unique ways, will produce great results.

If a traditional organization chart for the operational aspects of a city were to be drawn, the City Manager would be at the top of that chart. That fact alone makes the City Manager a leader. Whether the person who fills the box on the organization chart is a good leader or an effective leader are totally different questions. The point is this: City Managers must envision themselves as leaders. They must understand leadership and develop the skills necessary to be both good and effective in their leadership responsibilities because leadership is the first duty of a City Manager.

In this section, I'm going to talk about leadership, what it is and what it isn't. I'll explain the characteristics of a good leader and elaborate on what it takes to be an effective leader. At the end of this section, the reader will better understand the foundation of how to lead a city. Keep in mind, however, learning to fully understand and apply leadership principles is the work of a lifetime.

What is Leadership?

This is a simple but vital question. Like so many simple things, it may not be easy. Smart and experienced people have tried for a long time to express what leadership really is. There are many answers to the question. I was once told by an important mentor that leadership is like a large mansion with many rooms. By analogy, the mansion is leadership. The rooms represent different definitions and dimensions of leadership. All rooms taken together make up the mansion of leadership; each room taken separately is incomplete. The mansion is too big, too complex, to adequately describe in a single phrase or word.

Here is my best effort at describing what leadership is: Whenever I think of leadership, in my mind's eye I envision a squad of soldiers hunkered down in a foxhole. One of them jumps up and yells, "Follow me!" And they do. A leader is driven by core values and has a clear vision of the mission. A leader has the courage, drive, and skill to do something about it. A leader knows where to go, how to get there and is willing to take necessary calculated risks. A leader has the experience, ability, and moral authority to command the respect of other people. A leader can motivate people to action, and gets things done. If the initiative fails, and the leader lives through it, he will stand up and take responsibility for what he did. If the initiative succeeds, he will spread the credit to all the squad members. This is the essence of leadership, on the battlefield or in the city organization.

Further, it has been helpful for me to think of the source of leadership as being either by authority or by influence. For all but one of my work experiences, my leadership was based in authority. People did what I asked them to do because I was at the top of the organization chart; some document, like a city charter, said I had authority to tell them what to do. If they didn't obey, they could be disciplined or fired. However, when I was County Administrator in Polk County, Iowa, I had no such authority. All the executive authority in that county rested with the Board of Supervisors, not the County Administrator. Half of the department heads were independently elected and fiercely independent. The other half had a strong connection with, if not political protection from, at least one the members of the Board Supervisors. It was there that I learned that I didn't need authority to be a leader, but in the absence of authority, I did need influence. I needed to demonstrate that I: 1) was professionally competent, 2) practiced professional conduct, 3) maintained moral authority, 4) was reasonable, 5) was not politically motivated, 6) was clear about expectations. I needed to show them that they would be more successful by following me than by doing it another way. Leadership by influence takes patience and long-suffering; it takes kindness; it takes putting the best interest of the people you lead ahead of self interest in accomplishing the organizational objectives. In short, I needed to align myself so that people respected what I said and were willing to comply with my requests because I couldn't order them to do anything. This is leadership by influence. It is powerful when done right. There is, of course, nothing that would prevent someone who has authority from practicing leadership by influence as well.

I remember an experience I had while serving in the Army. I was a young buck sergeant leading a team of subordinate soldiers. I asked one of them, "Will you do such and such?" His answer was, "No." It took me back a little. What I had asked him to do was part of the job and it wasn't unreasonable. However, I had no personal influence with him so he wasn't going to willingly comply with my request. I said, "Let me rephrase that... You will do such and such." He complied immediately to the authoritative order. He respected my positional authority but not my personal influence.

Here is another leadership truth: I've never met a good leader who wasn't first a good follower. The two are not mutually exclusive; there is nothing that prevents a person from being both a leader and a follower at the same time. The City Manager, for example, is both a leader of subordinates and a follower of the City Council. Additionally, there are always informal leaders in every organization, like union leaders for example, who have no formal position authority in the organization but have great influence. In professional circles, more should be said about followership.

Followership is the process of willingly upholding the leader. That doesn't necessarily mean blindly following; it does mean supporting, contributing and working to help the boss and mission be successful. A leader is ineffective and useless without successful people who follow. Followership is an art and skill equal in importance to leadership. There was a time when soldiers in state-formed military units elected their own leaders. In our national, state and local political jurisdictions, we elect our leaders. In clubs and non-profit organizations, we elect our leaders. In all these institutions, we choose who we will follow. I submit that it is always the case that followers choose who they will follow. Even in situations where we don't agree with the leader who was chosen, we make up our own mind to follow or not. Those who choose to not follow will stonewall, deflect and make leadership difficult. When followers reject a chosen leader's authority, they must be won over through influence. If the leader cannot win them over through influence, failure waits at the doorstep because all that's left is authority and authority alone has severe limitations.

You can see from the thoughts so far expressed that leadership has everything to do with people: guiding them, motivating, influencing, and helping them. Leadership is personal; leadership is people work.

Here is another leadership truth that I have learned over the years: An organization will eventually begin to act like and take on the characteristics of its leader. If the leader is slothful, immoral or tolerates mediocrity, so also will the organization. If the leader is ethical, professional, and competent, so also will be the organization. Unfortunately, many of the requisite characteristics of good leadership are not easily tested for and are not easy to discern; so that selecting good leaders for the organization is not an easy task. Those responsible for selecting leaders in an organization should thoroughly understand leadership and be very careful about their selections. The screening and testing process in most cities deals with technical competence, not leadership ability. I got to the point in my career that when I was required to make a hiring decision, I rarely asked technical questions. I rightly assumed that the testing and screening process done by Human Resources or other recruiting specialist would bring me technically competent people. I remember one specific candidate I interviewed for a department head position. He complained that my questions were unexpected and difficult. My interview questions always dealt with leadership qualities and leadership character. I wanted people in the organization to reflect the best of leadership, as I understood it.

Leadership means being out front. Because the City Manager is the Chief Executive Officer of the municipal corporation, he or she is always out front and, by definition, always a leader. It may be argued whether a City Manager is a good or bad, an effective or ineffective leader. It cannot, however, be questioned that the City Manager is always a leader.

What is a "Good" Leader?

Let's be clear. There are good leaders and there are effective leaders. They are not necessarily the same thing. To explain, I will use the traditional view of two well-known leaders as examples: George Washington and Adolf Hitler. Both were effective leaders. They stood at the head of their respective countries; they had a vision for where their countries should go; they translated that vision into action, they modeled behavior; they motivated people to join their cause and people followed them. Both were effective leaders.

"Effective" gets the job done. "Good" implies values.

I understand that, when dealing with values, there is a substantial degree of subjectivity and interpretation involved. What is right and what is wrong? What is good and what not so good, or even bad? From my perspective, the meaning of "good" is this: good respects people and life. Good holds diversity, individuality and freedom of choice in high regard. Good is disciplined and self-sufficient but also benevolent, kind and does not neglect the needs of others. Good is ethical and principled; there are lines that good simply will not cross. Good is confident but not conceited. Good works hard but understands its own limitations and trusts in the goodness of others and the providence of the universe. One cannot be a good leader without first being a good person. George Washington was a good leader; Adolph Hitler was not. Feel free to substitute your own examples to illustrate the point.

Good leaders will model good values and character traits from the top of the organization. Good followers will seek out leaders that possess good traits and choose to follow them. If the leaders do not possess good traits, some of the employees will leave the organization to seek good leadership elsewhere. Other employees will simply stonewall a bad leader and try to outlast the regime. The selection of new employees by the leader will naturally better fit the leadership style of the new leader. All of this promotes the process of the organization eventually looking like its leader.

One City Manager that I knew and observed had an indirect communication style. Rather than kindly and directly confronting subordinates regarding their shortcomings or clearly stating what his expectations of them were, he simply made the work environment for them as uncomfortable as possible in the hope that they would "see the handwriting on the wall" and voluntarily leave. Even though many managers utilize this style, I consider it to be very bad practice. It is not ethical; it borders on dishonesty. It neither values nor helps people. One of the department heads in that same city was a very good leader and competent in his responsibilities, but he did not fit the new Manager's overall leadership style. It was only a few short months before he left to find work in another location that better fit his personal values and professional ethics. Over the course of my career, I actually hired a number of good department heads that were searching for new jobs because of leadership incompatibility with their previous bosses.

Ethical behavior is a big part of good leadership. Much is said in professional organizations about ethics. Much is done to establish ethical standards and enforce those standards in professional organizations. The same is true in the City Manager's professional organization, the International City/County Management Association (ICMA). Most states have an ethics code in their state statutes and many cities have adopted ethics ordinances. For cities with ethics ordinances, it is common to have an Ethics Commission to oversee the ordinance, hear and judge charges of violations of the ordinance and recommend appropriate actions for maintaining ethical discipline. Most ethics ordinances are many pages long, 25, 50 or 75 pages long. They are full of definitions, expectations, requirements and exceptions. Exceptions are necessary because life is complicated. The problem with lengthy, detailed or complicated ethics ordinances is that when people read them, they too often look for ways to technically comply but act unethically. It's like the three truck drivers who were being interviewed for a job. They were asked to describe their skill by explaining how closely they could drive their truck to the edge of a cliff without going over. One driver said he could get within two feet of the edge. Another said she could get within a foot. A third driver said he would stay as far away from the edge of the cliff as possible. The third driver got the job. So it is with ethics. Ordinances should be designed to keep people away from the edge and people should stay as far away from ethical violations as possible. They should not look for technical compliance while skipping over the intent of ethical behavior. Lengthy, detailed and complicated ethics ordinances help people look for ways to get close to the edge.

From a pragmatic perspective, I have come to view ethics as the application of five basic principles. They are things that most people were taught by their parents before they went to the first grade but, like many simple things of great value, they take a lifetime of vigilant practice to master. They are:

1. <u>Be Honest</u>. Live by the rules. Follow the law. Don't short-change your obligation. Don't steal. Don't cheat. Don't take unfair advantage. Expel fraud from your life; be genuine.
2. <u>Be Fair</u>. In every situation, treat people at least as well as you would want to be treated in the same circumstances. Avoid conflicts of interest. Balance justice and mercy; if you must choose between them, be generous.
3. <u>Tell the Truth</u>. This is more than an absence of lying. This is an absence of deception and misdirection of every kind. It is transparency, candor and complete veraciousness.
4. <u>Keep Your Word</u>. When you say you will do something, do it. Be careful about giving your word in the first place; but, once given, faithfully follow through.
5. <u>Act with Integrity</u>. Live ethically, not because your boss expects it but because it is who you are. In the absence of clear guidelines, use your own moral compass to do the "right" thing, even if you're the only one who knows about it. Do the right thing even if it's embarrassing or it costs you money or you will lose your job over it. If you make a mistake, own it.

These are lofty concepts, and they are just words until tested by opposition. It is relatively easy to be ethical when nothing is at stake. Situations where money or job may be lost can truly test a person's ethical integrity. Without the opposition, without the decisions that test our commitment to the five principles, ethics are unnecessary. Opposition makes ethics real.

I recall an experience that demonstrates the application of some of the ethical principles I have outlined. Early in my career, I served in a dual position as Finance Director and Assistant City Manager. When my boss, the City Manager, left to take another job and on his recommendation, the City Council appointed me as City Manager. My boss had been loved and well respected by the City Council; they hated to see him leave. Two of the five members of the Council were very good friends with him. Their families even conducted social activities together. The two Councilmembers who were so close to the former Manager stayed in contact with him after he left. Within several weeks of his leaving, they approached me prior to the beginning of a weekly City Council meeting. They asked me to step into a vacant room because they had something private to say to me. They told me that the former Manager wanted to come back. They wanted me to step down from my newly appointed position so they could reappoint him. They said they intended to create a lucrative new job, Economic Development Director. They offered me the new job if I would step down as City Manager. When they saw my confusion and hesitation, they said that, if I didn't take their offer, they had the votes to fire me and that they would do so when the meeting started, just minutes away. When I rebounded from the initial shock, I told them that I needed a few moments to consider it. They agreed and stepped out of the room. I stayed and paced the floor, saying a silent prayer for guidance. When they returned, I told them that I would not step down. If they had the votes to fire me, they would need to exercise them. I was on edge as the meeting began. Nowadays they would have had to place the item on the agenda in advance to meet the requirements of open meeting laws, but not back then. They brought the subject up, but they did not have the third vote necessary to pass the motion. As if anticipating the failure of their motion, they immediately countered with a new proposal to bring the former Manager back into the Economic Development Director position which, they said, would be equal to the City Manager and report directly to the City Council. Although the entire situation was uncomfortable for me, I had to remind the Council that the ordinance that created the position of City Manager required that all administrative positions in the city report to the City Manager and not the City Council; if they were committed to creating the position, it would need to report to me. The issue finally died after the former Manager declined to accept the job offer. In fairness, he later told me that none of it was his idea. Such was my first real introduction to city management politics and ethics.

Cities, like other large organizations, have situations occur that erode public confidence and detract from their mission. A mechanic, for example, steals parts from the motor pool, a police officer exercises unnecessary force, a department head makes a commitment at a public meeting and then fails to deliver on the promise. A million things can go wrong. Every time I have experienced a situation that eroded public trust in my city, the heart of the problems has been a failure to live by one of the five ethical principles.

Here's another consideration regarding promoting ethics in a meaningful way: nobody's perfect. Our own failures, or fear of being criticized for our perceived hypocrisy, prevents us, generally, from being bold about ethical issues. It is hard to advocate high ethical behavior when you know that, somewhere along the line, you have fallen short. We all need to get past our own shortcomings, do our reasonable best to live ethically and understand that our best effort must be good enough. By doing this, we can help those that work for us to do the same. The world will be an ethically better place.

On an occasion after I had applied for a new City Manager position, I was selected as a semi-finalist and was asked to participate in several tests and evaluations to examine my suitability for the position. The city had hired a selection consultant that was also an industrial psychologist. He administered a battery of tests and then conducted a role-playing exercise to test his hypothesis about the candidates. One of his conclusions about me was that "he cannot lie." This is, of course, untrue in an absolute sense. Everyone lies. The better question is, how much does a person lie? Nevertheless, that is what he told the City Council. This was an important character trait for the City Council to consider because of their previous experience. Someone on the Council, predictably, passed that information on to the press, who published it for everyone to read. After I was hired and although I certainly tried to act in an honest and truthful way, this perception and expectation always made me feel uncomfortable.

I recall another experience. After working in a certain city for several years, I had gained a reputation of being a fair-minded manager. I was approached by a former employee who had a grievance with how his retirement was being handled. He had talked to previous city officials about it before talking to me. As he approached me, he said, "I have heard that you are a fair man...". Although I was glad for the reputation and the compliment, it made me uncomfortable because I knew that, from his perspective, he wanted me to side with his position on his grievance. I listened to his concerns and claims and researched all the facts, policies and laws. My conclusion was that his grievance was not valid. I communicated the same to him. He was, of course, disappointed. He no longer thought that I was fair. That was many years ago and the fact that he judged me to be unfair still bothers me. These types of practical concerns about other's judgement of our own behavior make the active promotion and the administration of ethical standards difficult and scary for leaders. But, if they neglect or defer it, they will have an even greater problem in public life.

For good leadership to exist, personal character is key. When I selected someone for a leadership position within my organization, character became the number one selection criteria. It trumps every other consideration. The selection consultant or Human Resources Department screened candidates for their knowledge, skills and abilities. They always made sure the candidate had the right experience and was technically suited for the job; I never had to worry about that part of the process. Character is much harder to evaluate and test for, however. Knowing the kind of personal character wanted and needed in a position is critical. Getting an accurate read on a candidate's character takes insight and intuition; it takes discernment beyond what can be seen on paper or even with your eyes. The best leaders I have hired over the course of my career were the ones that proved out to have the best character.

There is a lesson here for City Councils as well. The most important decision a City Council will make is whom they will hire as their City Manager. They need to get it right. More attention needs to be given to leadership and the values and character that are the foundation of good leadership. Like Samuel, the Old Testament prophet who was sent to find a replacement for Saul to be a king for Israel, we can't allow ourselves to be dazzled by outward appearance, fluff and showmanship, or candidate pandering. We must discern the heart, the core values and good leadership capacity of the candidate.

There is a lesson here for citizen voters as well. Too many times I have watched the electorate respond to City Council candidates who falsely speak of issues about which voters are passionate. Some candidates are very astute at discerning what voters want to hear. Those candidates "tickle the ears" of voters by telling them what they want to hear rather than the truth about the facts and alternatives. It isn't good enough to simply elect an outspoken candidate who will go down to City Hall and "give those people what for." Voters need to look more deeply into the values and character of candidates so that they can choose good Council members who are also good leaders. They, in turn, will pick good leaders who report to the City Council.

Ego and pride are among the stumbling blocks of character. Character is the substance of which good leaders are made. Political positions are magnets for people who have big egos. Voters should be very discerning about the leaders they elect. Character matters.

What are the Characteristics of a Good, Effective City Leader?

Allowing the analogy, leadership is like a large mansion with many rooms. All the rooms are important to the status of the mansion, even though some of the rooms are larger and perhaps more ornate than others. Some of the rooms represent characteristics that may be inherent, such as intelligence. You either have it or you don't. Others of the characteristics are learned through experience and practice. Let's move on to explore a few of the rooms that I believe are most critical for City Managers:

Intelligence

As I am referring to this characteristic, keep in mind that intelligence is not the totality of facts people are in possession of or the level of education attained. It is the speed and effectiveness level at which a person receives and processes information; the ability to relate divergent facts, perceive beyond the obvious and think abstractly. It is difficult to think strategically without high intelligence. The best leaders are very intelligent people.

In one of the cities I managed, we wanted to build our management team and enhance their leadership skills. To assist in that effort, we brought in an expert to assess our communications styles, management skills and leadership characteristics, including intelligence. With that information, we hoped to focus our training efforts on the areas that would most improve our performance as a team. All the management team were highly intelligent people, with one exception. This particular department head was, surprisingly, of average intelligence. He was one of the most successful and capable of all the department heads; he could always be counted on to get the job done well. When I inquired of the consultant to explain how this could be, I was told that concentration on one subject and repetition over a long period of time could imitate intelligence. While it was true that this department head may not have been as valuable to the team for brainstorming strategic direction, he remained an extremely valuable and competent team member in managing his department.

One of my department heads in another city had intelligence, based on scientific testing, that was off the charts high. I could always count on him to come up with "out of the box" ideas for the problems we were facing. Occasionally he was a little smug and he was intimidating for most of the people with whom he worked. One day, one of the other department heads asked me when I was going to fire him because his ideas, according to this second department head, were impractical and useless. The first department head had offended the second one with some off the wall thinking but I found merit in having different perspectives, even if they were wild ideas. It helped me see all sides of the issue even if, in the end, I didn't agree. I told the complaining department head that I had no intention of firing him; in fact, if I didn't have a personality like him on the team, I would go out and find one because it made the team stronger. Seeing things differently is a talent, often requiring high intelligence.

My conclusions: Hire highly intelligent people because intelligence is key to leadership, even if they are smarter than you. Get the facts before you act; never automatically dismiss anyone; there are exceptions to the rule. The generality still holds true: intelligence is key to leadership.

Confidence

Confident leaders are sure of themselves because they know themselves. They know their strengths and they know their weaknesses; they know what they know and they will admit what they don't know. They will build on their strengths and they will use the strengths of other people to cover their own weakness until they can improve themselves. They recognize calculated risk and approach it reasonably. Confident leaders know their jobs and rely on the lessons they have learned through experience to avoid making the same mistake twice. Ego, arrogance and boastfulness are imitations of confidence. In fact, these latter traits oftentimes mask a lack of true confidence. When selecting new leaders for the organization, be very careful to not confuse the imitations for the real deal.

Trustworthiness

When I was in graduate school, one of my professors asked the question, "What is the primary function of a manager?". After many answers and much discussion, his answer was, "To get the job done." My professor was a well-recognized academic as well as an elected official.

I remember a similar conversation among my colleagues in a Texas city. The topic was trust: What is trust and what is its practical application in city management? Their conclusion was that it all boiled down to whether you could be confident that a person would do their job. Their analogy was a military one. In the army, they said, there are people of varied, and sometimes incompatible, value systems. Their values make no difference. In the end, all that matters is that you can count on the other person to be at the right place, at the right time, to fulfill the assigned mission. That part of the discussion was interesting to me because none of them had ever served in a military unit. I might agree that some personal values are irrelevant to the workplace; but completely disagree that trust is without value. I thought that their discussion was shallow and simply didn't go far enough. More questions should have been asked. For example, what is it that motivates the soldier to be at the right place; to do the right thing? What makes one confident that the soldier will obey his superiors when their orders put his life on the line? Could it be fear? Fear of punishment; fear of authority? I think that could be part of it. Fear can motivate in the short run but it cannot maintain long term performance; it cannot spawn consistent creativity. I maintain that trust is the personal quality that ensures that leaders will be followed. It is trust that ensures consistent organizational performance and creative excellence. Trust is founded on the leader's ethical behavior and the follower's confidence in that behavior.

Both examples cited above, the one from my graduate school and the one from Texas, are missing something important. Sustained superior performance depends, not only on getting the job done, but also on the trust that underlies the action. The motives and values that drive accomplishment are of equal importance to accomplishing the task itself. Ethical behavior is key to trust. Trust is key to good leadership and sustained performance. The ends do not always justify the means; focusing only on the outcome is an incomplete concept. The soldier must know that her orders have purpose and come from people who have integrity, who would never needlessly put her life in danger, who would, and have, obeyed life-threatening orders themselves. Trust is deeper than the result. It is assured reliance on the character, ability, ethics and integrity of a person. It is not the mission that moves the organization; it is trust.

A leader who is trustworthy is one who can be relied upon to get the job done in a professional, competent, ethical way. Leaders at the top of the city's organization chart must be worthy of trust, must have ethical integrity. If not, they will eventually be leading a morally bankrupt organization and they will lose the confidence of the people; they will deserve the cynicism that will, inevitably, be heaped upon them.

Trust is like a governor on an engine. An engine governor restricts the engine to lower levels of performance by keeping its RPMs below a certain number. Without trust, you will be able to take your organization only so far and only so fast. If your tax-paying constituency doesn't trust you, you will be road--blocked. If your workforce doesn't trust you, you will be stonewalled. If your boss, the City Council, doesn't trust you, you will be fired. After establishing trust, you will be amazed at what you can accomplish.

A final thought: Trust is a precious commodity to possess. It should be vigorously guarded and protected. However, we are all human and I know no persons who haven't broken trust to one degree or another in either their professional or personal life. It is important to know that broken trust can be rebuilt. I'm not saying that it is easy, but it can be done.

Communications

It is one thing for a leader to know where the organization should be going and the methods by which it should get there; it is another thing for everyone else to know it. As previously noted, leadership is people work. The ability to communicate is central to working with people.

By definition and in reality, leaders stand at the front. People look to them for guidance and direction. Some of the primary functions of leadership are to set direction and to clarify expectations. It follows then, that the more leaders communicate and clarify, the better off everyone will be.

Another benefit of communication is that it allows people to act for themselves, to use their own creativity and problem-solving skills to contribute to the mission of the organization. This is far better and more organizationally mature than telling everyone exactly what they should do for every task. I have been in organizations where people were very willing to do whatever they were told but were unwilling to do anything that they were not told to do. This type of organization is very inefficient. Don't get me wrong; there is a place for a "top-down" style such as in disaster or turn-around management. It is not, however, good for developing sustained excellent performance.

It is impossible for leaders to anticipate every condition or circumstance and, therefore, impossible to communicate specific directions on every detail. People need to be given general clarification of their mission and desired outcomes and then allowed to use their own skills to achieve the end product. In the military, they call it "commander's intent".

I recall a lesson I learned. We had been receiving complaints about the poor maintenance at our main city park such as lack of sufficient irrigation, long intervals between grass cutting, not enough trimming, etc. It was the location for all the youth sports for our city and it got a lot of use. As soon as we could, we began experimenting with putting flower beds at the entrances to the park. You wouldn't believe the many positive comments we received about how well we were maintaining the park; it was a complete turn-around! Nothing had changed, except the addition of two flower beds. I made it clear to the Parks Superintendent that I wanted more flowers at various locations around the city. His first reaction was that it was too costly, and he would need more budget. Sorry, no more budget. To my mild surprise, the next spring there were flower beds popping up throughout the city. I learned that the Parks Superintendent had managed his budget from the previous year carefully and saved enough to build a small greenhouse to grow flowers from seed rather than purchase them ready to plant. The Superintendent understood the intent and expectations; he found a creative, relatively inexpensive, solution that lasted for many years. This experience helped form a big part of my management style for the balance of my career.

Here is another experience to demonstrate the importance of communication. On one occasion when I was going to be out of town, I left an Assistant City Manager in charge. When I returned, I received a lot of positive feedback from Councilmembers that she had done a good job. I was not surprised that she had done a good job, but I wanted to know more precisely what she had done to earn the unsolicited praise from the City Council. It was simple. She had spent a lot of time keeping them informed while I was gone. The Council had confidence because they knew what was going on and that someone was dealing with the issues. Her methods were different than mine, but they worked well for her and the incident reinforced the importance of communicating more rather than less.

Here's another example. We were in contract negotiations with one of the employee unions. The Union had a long history of getting everything it wanted, even though some of it was unreasonable. Their strategy, which had worked for them for many, many years was to divide the City Council from the management team. They did that by going to the City Council privately and individually to tell the Councilmembers how mean and unfair the negotiating team was being. Historically, the City Council would eventually break down and direct the City Manager to settle the contract. When I faced my first contract renewal in this city, my tenured staff counseled me to just give them what they wanted and be done with it rather than go through the pain of negotiating because the Council would, in the end, give them what they wanted anyway. That was unacceptable to me. In fact, it was so important to me that the negotiating process work that I had to replace the city's traditional chief negotiator. He had been through the process so many times and "lost;" he had the wrong mindset. As the negotiations moved forward, the management/negotiating team reported progress to the City Council every week. Additionally, we videotaped the negotiating sessions and made them available to the Council and public over our cable TV channel. This transparent communication, along with other professional union negotiating techniques, broke the historical precedent and solved the problem; it led to a fair and mutually acceptable contract.

Communication is key to good leadership.

Approachableness

Because leadership in city management is "people business," people need to feel like they can talk to their leader. Admittedly, caution needs to be exercised to prevent the chain of command from being ineffective or to prevent the unnecessary consumption of all the leader's time. A balance and process must be found so that the leader is approachable. I have used open door policies, hot lines, management by walking around, department or division meetings with Q&A sessions, neighborhood meetings, speaking engagements, hanging around the City Council chambers to talk to people before and after meetings and other techniques, to emphasize my approachability. One of my respected City Manager colleagues would have a birthday luncheon once per month for all employees that had a birthday during that month. He would make sure that he spent one-on-one time with each of the people attending. That technique wouldn't work in every city or for every City Manager, but it worked for him.

Predictability

It helps followers a great deal to know what is expected of them, to be able to anticipate their leader's requirements and reaction. This is especially true in emergency situations. When I took a new job, I found it helpful to meet with staff and talk about myself. Truly, that was uncomfortable for me because it felt overly ego centric, but I didn't mean it in that way. I simply wanted staff to know who they were working for, to let them peer into my brain to see how I thought and how I evaluated, to anticipate my reactions and requirements. It was a "quick start" to working together and it helped them feel much more at ease with a new and unknown boss. That type of dialog continued in our weekly staff meetings where we would always have an "after action" review of our City Council meetings. We talked about why things happened the way they did, about how we could have done things differently, about what we would do next time that same circumstance arose. It was very helpful for everyone and good training for my department heads. They learned my thinking process and it helped make them much more confident.

Steadiness

Being "steady" is also important. By steady I mean not over-reacting to things. I spent my entire career trying to keep my emotions under control. Don't get me wrong, I think it's good for staff to see that you can occasionally get mad, but, unless it is your intent to lead by fear and intimidation, it should be a rare occurrence. The regular flaring of emotion impedes the work; it gets in the way of people acting with creativity and confidence. In one of my cities, I had an Assistant who had a hard time controlling his emotions. Something unexpected or challenging would happen and his emotions would flare. He would raise his voice

41

and be accusatory. After some coaching, he tried to not flare, but his complexion would turn bright red starting at his neckline and go up past his ears to his forehead. It was easy for staff to see his emotion boiling over, even if he didn't say anything. It terrified them as they anticipated an emotional outburst. It was a real challenge to his career.

Responsibility

Good leaders take initiative, and they take responsibility. They anticipate needs; they resolve problems before they occur. When things don't go as planned, they step up and acknowledge their shortcoming rather than shifting blame. Blame-shifters are poor leaders. They are probably in a position that is more responsible than their abilities would justify. If they work for you, you should watch them closely and consider demoting them to a more technical position rather than one with heavy leadership requirements.

On one occasion, I worked with a department manager who, on paper, was well qualified for the job but he was a weak leader. Because the city was in a high growth mode, there was a lot of activity in his area of responsibility. The local developers were aggressive and politically active. There was always conflict about zoning proposals and development requirements, for both the current as well as long-term. Something was always going wrong. These conditions will sound familiar to any City Manager who has worked in a high growth city. In this example, however, the manager was a blame-shifter. From his point of view, any time there was a problem, it was because one of the staff had failed at a task, or he had not received the budget he needed to hire another needed person, or the City Council had failed to support him on a previously proposed code amendment that would have fixed the problem, or he had tried a solution before and failed to get necessary support so he wouldn't try it again; or. or…or… For the good of the city, he eventually had to be replaced. In another city with similar growth challenges, the department leader took responsibility and found solutions to the challenges. He held listening sessions with developers, builders and staff members and then made reasonable changes to departmental processes and policies. He held code training sessions for staff and then for developers. He attended Builder's Association meetings to make himself available for comments and questions. He professionally and fairly replaced problematic staff members. He turned the conflicts from a roaring fire to a flickering flame. When something went wrong, he acknowledged it and did something about it. He was a leader.

This problem is not limited to department heads and subordinate leaders in a city. Although rare, I have also known City Managers who placed subordinates between themselves and difficult problems so that they would have someone to blame if it didn't turn out well. Worse than that, they would intentionally place disfavored subordinates in positions to fail so that it would be easier to get rid of them. Then to put bitter icing on that distasteful cake, they considered themselves very clever to have managed in that manner. Shame on them. City Councils, take note and fix that problem if it happens in your city. I was fortunate to have been able to hire several good department heads who had been treated this way by previous bosses.

Here's another personal example about taking responsibility. When I was in Corpus Christi, we had issues with our water quality and with the water lines in our system. The system was old. It had a lot of ductile iron in it, which developed bacteria more frequently. There were a lot of dead-end lines that needed to be flushed more frequently. There were many private wells that had inadequate backflow protection. To top it off, at certain times of the year, the agricultural land discharged a lot of fertilizer into the Nueces River which was one of the primary sources of the city's potable water. The fertilizer nitrates were very difficult to remove through the treatment process. When they passed through into the old distribution system, they helped the bacteria to grow. The Safe Drinking Water Act requires a certain level of testing be done in every public water system to ensure high quality. If the tests don't meet specific standards, orders are given to boil culinary water before it is used for consumption. Some of these problems could be reduced by hyper-injecting more chlorine into the treatment process, and that resulted in many more public complaints about the odor and taste of the water. One year was particularly bad. We had already had two city-wide boil orders. When we had the third, there was a public uproar. The water system was a difficult problem. I felt like we had taken reasonable steps to address it, but here we were with a third city-wide boil order within a year's time. The public was justifiably angry. I knew that all I had to do to deflect the anger was to offer up a sacrifice and fire someone. I had fired plenty of people. There was professional necessity for those firings. I couldn't justify this one without becoming a blame-shifter myself. That was not the kind of leadership I had spent a career practicing. So, after a long weekend of soul-searching, I resigned. There were many in the city who objected and said that I was not responsible for the failures in the water system, but I was. My position was at the top of the organization chart and that made me responsible for everything that happened inside of the organization. Our water system had failed three times that year and it was time for a leader to take responsibility.

Decision-Making

Knowing how and when to make a decision is critical for leaders. When I was in graduate school, one of my professors diverted from the normal course curriculum to talk about how to make decisions. At the time I wondered why we were spending the time away from our normal subject. Since then, I have thought that it might have been one of the most important classes I had in graduate school. He started his lesson by using an automobile wheel as an example. He asked us to describe wheel. We started out saying it was round and of a certain height and width. We ended up talking about the tire, the metal rim, the lug nuts; the type of tire, belted or radial, etc.; the number of lug nuts, their configuration and threading; the rim, size, width, composition, metal plating, powder coating. And much more. There were more details and information that came out of the discussion of a single automobile wheel than I had ever first imagined. His point: you need to understand a problem before you can make decisions about solving it. You need all the information and all the facts before you can make a good decision. There are always many alternatives to any given problem, and you need to know what they are. There are costs involved. There are costs to each of the alternative solutions and there are costs to doing nothing at all. Following graduate school, I learned that all decisions have political and organizational impacts as well. They, too, must be anticipated. All these things must be known before good decisions can be made. I have long since learned that a problem well defined is a problem mostly resolved. This seems self-evident, so does this detail really make a difference? I will answer that question with another simple question: Were there really weapons of mass destruction in Iraq? In the city business, you would be surprised at how often leaders jump to conclusions before all the facts are known. Do your due diligence before you decide. It matters.

It takes time to gather Information for decision-making. Long-term City Planners have time to evaluate before they make their decisions. A SWAT commander must make split-second decisions. My point is that all decisions have a timeframe and good decisions will be made inside of that timeframe. Some decisions must be made, even if there is more information that would be nice to have. My rule of thumb is that City Managers should make decisions as quickly as possible without compromising reasonable due diligence. Unnecessarily delaying a decision will cause frustration for followers and for superior leaders as well.

Over the years, several of my Assistant City Managers have been former Police Chiefs. I am recalling one who was a very good manager and leader. He was a good decision-maker, but he tended to make decisions faster than necessary, which meant that not all the needed information was always gathered. I think it was a leftover trait from his many years in police work where necessary snap decisions were common. He initially was frustrated with me for asking due diligence questions and slowing the decision-making process down but later acknowledged that one of the best lessons he learned from me was how to make better decisions.

Courage

Working in the public sector as a City Manager takes courage. Speaking truth to power is a constant, not only with the City Council but with the public at large, many of whom are quick to remind you that they pay your salary. Unlike the private sector where there is a profit motive to help make some of the most difficult decisions, there is none in the public sector. There is only the integrity of the leaders to prevent unreasonable compromise. Union contracts are an example. I have seen instances where union leaders have gone after City Managers to personally attack their integrity or try to get them fired to intimidate their way into a favorable contract. The threat of a vote of no-confidence is a powerful union tool.

When a leader has nothing to gain and everything to lose, it takes courage to do the right thing. I recall an incident when a potential candidate for City Council came into my office to threaten me. He said, with animated conviction, that if I didn't take a favorable position on a development issue that was coming before the city, he would make sure, after he was elected, that I would be fired, and that he had the community backing from the right people to make it happen. It took courage to calmly and politely explain to him why my recommendation to the City Council would not be aligned with his desires. He left angry and I think determined to keep his word. The meeting was very stressful for me as was simply thinking about it afterward. As it turned out in this specific instance, the potential candidate was in an auto crash and unable to finish his bid for elected office. Unfortunately, this was not the only such experience I had that emphasized the need for courage.

Boldness

On one occasion after starting a new job, I interviewed all the people who reported directly to me. As part of the interview, I asked each employee what one thing was most important that I know or do. One of my direct reports gave me some very important, sage advice: Whenever you see something that you know needs to be done, do it. Don't shrink from it; just do it.

The advice proved to be invaluable and prophetic. To act when action is required, when others have shrunken from it because of the potentially negative political, legal, or other consequences, is BOLD. One of my first acts in that city was to fire one of the key department heads. It was clear that he needed to be replaced, and everyone knew it. Because of his influential position, because of political correctness and because he had been trained in the law, others had shied away from that decision. Even some members of the public, who talked to me afterward, considered the firing to be a bold and necessary move.

The opposite of bold is fainthearted and overcautious. I am not suggesting that caution be abandoned but that <u>over</u>-caution be abandoned.

There are many rooms in the leadership mansion. Although we've mentioned only ten of them here, I believe they are the most important ones for a City Manager. Here's some advice for elected officials who are responsible for selecting a City Manager. When you select someone to lead your city, look for these characteristics. Don't be fooled by a slick tongue in a schmoozed-up interview. It is common for elected officials, who themselves are generally smart, articulate, outgoing and vitally interested in the welfare of their community, to be tasked with selecting the top leader for their city. It takes a good leader to choose a good leader, and it's easy to make a mistake because the important characteristics are not always readily apparent. Be careful. Know what you're looking for. All your background screening and interview questions should be strategically directed at discovering these characteristics.

Now that we've talked about the characteristics of, and the foundation principles that make up, good city leaders, let's talk about what leaders do.

What do Leaders do?

So far, we have established that 1) organizations have leaders; 2) those leaders affect individual performance; and 3) good leaders have characteristics that can be defined. Consider everything we've talked about so far as the first floor of the mansion. Now, let's move on to the second floor and talk about what it is that leaders do. Like the first floor, the second floor also has many rooms. I want to explore here just seven of those rooms. The characteristics and skills represented by these rooms make a big difference in the performance of cities. City Managers who have the leadership skills of these seven rooms will serve their city's by providing:

Vision

Leaders articulate a vision for their organization. They see what is and they project what can be. They know where they want to end up. They are not satisfied to coast along; they strive for improvement; they strive for excellence. The future they see challenges people; it excites them. I think of President Kennedy saying in 1961, that the United States would put a man safely on the moon before the end of the decade. That was vision. It was bold, it was challenging, it was inspiring.

I recall observing a large industry that was close to bankruptcy. The historical leadership had done all it could to make the company successful but to no avail. That company was about to follow so many others in its sector into complete failure. Then the company was taken over by a partnership led by experienced people with a new vision for the company. It was a vision of success and prosperity. Where others saw failure, they saw opportunity. To the outside observer, like me, the required actions they took were difficult and painful, but through tough-minded, expert leadership, they succeeded. Their vision turned into reality; the company was not only saved but it prospered. This observation taught me a great lesson and I used it thereafter in the cities that I managed.

Earlier in my career, it was in vogue for cities to write and publish vision and mission statements. I think the trend came from then-current management theory and popular books that were being published. It made sense to have such statements but, in most cities, they took on a surreal tone that was hollow in meaning but flowery in language. In the end, it didn't get cities noticeably closer to excellence because it was more poetry than substance. Like the moon landing and the failing company, wishing it so does not make it so. Along with vision, you need to have a plan and the means to achieve the vision. Otherwise, the vision is only an entertaining, wishful dream.

Leaders combine a vision for the future with the means to achieve the vision. Otherwise, they are not the leaders who create and execute the game plan, but cheerleaders who support the actions of the team on the field.

When I was in Corpus Christi, Texas, my stated vision was for the city to become the best performing city in the State of Texas. I was serious about the vision; I had a plan to make it so. The plan included benchmarking performance in each functional area of the city, comparing those benchmarks to other cities and creating improvement plans to surpass the best performing ones.

It is also very helpful to integrate vision, mission and workplans into the Council's adopted policies. By doing so, it helps keep the entire city team, elected officials and staff, focused and in alignment.

Clarity

One of the most important duties of leaders is to provide clarity. They clarify vision; they clarify mission; and they clarify performance expectations.

Organizations work their very best when all the people in them are using all their skills, abilities, and creativity to accomplish their work. With a clear understanding of the vision, mission, and performance expectations, people can forge synergies from their own creativity. No leader is good enough to do all the thinking for the entire organization. No leader has the time to do everyone else's work for them. It is vital to performance excellence that everyone understand the mission, the ends, and performance expectations. All of this requires clarity. Creating clarity is hard work. It involves thinking a subject through in detail and boiling it down to its critical essence. It involves deciding what is acceptable and what is not acceptable. It involves deciding in advance when the organization will have arrived at its goals. It involves articulating the results of this difficult work and transferring those essential ideas into others' minds.

At one point, one of my city's departments sorely needed fixing. There was obvious customer dissatisfaction. There were rumors of corruption. The employees were lethargic, avoided dealing with critical issues and made a lot of excuses. There are, generally, two approaches to fixing a badly broken department: 1) fire everyone and start over or 2) fire the leader and let a new leader fix the problems. I had previously used both approaches and knew the advantages and disadvantages of each. I thought about this problem for days. At the end of the thinking, I chose the latter. I knew I would need a great change agent and I knew I would have to manage expectations all the way around. After finding the best change manager in the city, I reassigned him to the broken department. I knew that it would be a huge challenge. I knew that, even though we would maintain a strong sense of urgency, it would still take more time than I wanted. As part of my previous thinking, I had begun to write down precisely what I wanted accomplished in that department. I tried to be concise, direct and realistic. I wanted to be clear about what would satisfy me in changing the department's performance. I wanted the new manager to know exactly what I expected. I ended up with about a half of a page of bullet points, with a brief explanation for each point. When I proposed the assignment to the new manager, I covered the expectations in detail. I gave him a copy. I told him to think about it and I told him that, if he accepted the assignment, I wanted a plan from him about how he would accomplish the goals. I also wanted his plan attached to a timeline. After due consideration, he accepted the challenging assignment and he carried through with his plan. In about a year and a half, he had met all my expectations and completely turned the department around. I was very proud of his success.

Modeling Behavior

One of my profound observations over the course of my career is that an organization will, over time, take on the characteristics of its leader, for good or bad. It is a natural occurrence because the leaders at the top of the organizational chart will select, train and influence subordinate leaders who reflect their values, goals and methods. It is also true that leaders at the top, whether they intend to or not, act as models of behavior for the rest of the organization. By observation and reinforcement, subordinate leaders will try to please their boss by doing what they believe the boss expects; they will mimic behavior they observe from their leader. To have an excellent organization, leaders must model excellent behavior.

Shortly after taking a new job, I observed that one of the smaller departments was grossly underperforming. Performance measures were horrible, customer complaints were high and revenues were down. After taking a deeper dive into their performance and operations, it became clear that the personal lives of the leaders and employees were interfering with the accomplishment of their mission. There was a great deal of inappropriate fraternization occurring throughout the organization which dampened performance and placed the city at legal risk. The leader not only tolerated it but was a participant. Most members of the department followed his example. Although painful and difficult, my solution was a massive housecleaning and replacement of the managers with competent leaders who were focused on the mission.

A more productive example occurred in one of my police departments. The city charter required that the Chief be selected from within the department, ensuring that an experienced leader who was very familiar with the city get the job. The new Chief had an excellent reputation for competence and ethical behavior. He made it clear to the department that honesty and truthfulness were required of all officers. He had certainly modeled those principles for many years and had moral authority to reinforce that standard. On one occasion an officer committed a relatively minor work violation which would have normally earned a reprimand or a day off work. However, when confronted, the officer had been untruthful about it. The untruthfulness earned him a termination. Part of the Chief's rationale was that police officers go to court and give testimony; they must be believable. Dishonesty of any kind undermines public confidence and their ability to successfully do their job. He enforced the standard and modeled it from the top.

Motivation

Motivating people is a key function of leadership and there are many ways to do it. For example, authority, fear and intimidation are methods that motivate people, but they rarely inspire them. Love and persuasion can also motivate people, as can bribery and promised reward. Individuals are motivated by many different things such as duty, pride, professionalism, greed, self-interest, fear, love, hate, shame, peer pressure, etc. Leaders can appeal to all these emotions to get people to do things, but, from my point of view, using positive and uplifting motivating methods are always better than using negative ones. In fact, ethics requires it to be so, because there is a difference between manipulation and motivation, between persuasion and compulsion.

I recall an instance when we were trying to implement something new in a Police Department. They were resisting the change. As I was counseling with the department leadership about the issue, one of the Deputy Chiefs said, "We have to show the department what's in it for them." He was saying that the department needed to be better informed to understand the bigger picture; why it was not only good for the city but also good for them. In this case, they needed to be persuaded. At first, I didn't care for his comment because, from my perspective, people should have done the right thing simply because I thought it was good for the organization and not because there was something in it for them. He was correct though, in the sense that people are motivated by different factors. Within ethical boundaries, leaders must find what motivates people and use it to make needed change. In this instance, along with department leadership, we attended watch commander meeting and shift briefings to further explain the need for the change, demonstrate how it would benefit all concerned, and to answer the officer's questions. The process was slower than I liked, but it worked out successfully.

Leading significant change in an organization requires a special dimension of motivation; it requires a generally accepted sense of urgency. Initially, this may sound easier than it really is because 1) the urgency must be real; it cannot be phony and 2) it must be understood and believed by the followers before they will cooperate in the extraordinary effort necessary to change. When you're in the middle of a disaster, it's too late to prepare. You must prepare in advance and make necessary change to avoid or mitigate a catastrophic event. For reasons previously discussed, leaders generally anticipate problems before their followers, and they need to start solving the problems before they are well known. Successful solutions to the biggest problems require a sense of urgency.

Here's another example from a city that had operated a wastewater treatment plant for many years. We had received many complaints about its odor, how it was being operated and the rising cost of the monthly fees. We also received EPA notices of violation which were potentially very costly, only adding to the problems. It was clear to me that significant changes needed to be made but I ran into gross resistance from the people responsible for running the plant. They were convinced that they were working hard and doing everything they could to run the plant efficiently. Along with the Public Works Director, I did a lot of research on the operations of wastewater plants. We found out which ones in the State were being run most efficiently and cost effectively. We visited those plants and talked to their leaders. We did our due diligence. A significant fact we learned was that the most outstanding plants were being managed by private companies. After gaining political support by briefing the city Council on the financial issues and gaining their concurrence, I determined to outsource the operation of the plant. We hired a consulting engineer with experience in the field to draft bid documents for private companies to make proposals. The plant personnel were not happy with my decision. After everyone's emotions had cooled down, they persuaded me to let them make a competing proposal for the operation of the plant. The process turned into a managed competition rather than a straight-out outsourcing. The city even provided the internal team with some consulting engineering because we wanted to have confidence in the proposal that they intended to submit. In the end, the internal proposal won the sealed bid. They came up with the lowest cost proposal through introduction of new technology, upgrades for energy savings, and reduced staff costs through early retirement. It was a creative, fair, total-cost bid. All the proposals, including the internal one, included performance benchmarks, timelines and a contract. The winning internal proposal saved the city a little less than a million dollars per year, which was a significant number for back then. Without the urgent and real threat of outsourcing, the staff would not likely have had the motivation to make the significant changes necessary to improve plant operations. It became one of the top performing plants in the State.

Accountability

Leaders hold themselves, and others, accountable. The aim of leadership is to get people to act. Accountability is both a mind-set and process for making sure things happen. All the other leadership work either fails or becomes marginal if accountability is not introduced.

To be accountable, people must be clear on what they are accountable for. To expect otherwise is unfair and unrealistic. The task, goal, or performance expectation must be explicit, and it must be time-bound. Leaders are, therefore, required to do the hard work of determining specifically what they want to accomplish. Further, the object of their determination must become a shared expectation because, in most cases, other people will do the actual work.

Let me give a couple of examples of how I created accountability for myself and my direct reports in the city. First, are my 100-day Plans. I made my work time-bound by dividing it into 100-day increments. At the beginning of each new 100 days, I would establish a priority list of strategic goals I wanted to advance. The lists were relatively short. I would never give myself more than three things to accomplish and I would delegate no more than three to any one person because I was serious about seeing them accomplished. Experience taught me that a person who has one goal is much more likely to accomplish it than a person who has ten. I found that three goals are the maximum practical limit for getting things done. At the beginning of the 100 days, I would report to the City Council on the accomplishments of the previous 100 days and preview my plan for the upcoming 100 days. For goals that were delegated, I asked the responsible person to give me a detailed plan, breaking the goal down to actionable steps and attaching a timeline to each step. The process was very accountable, and it was surprising how much we really got done. The process had the additional benefit of helping the City Council be informed about what I was working on in the organization. I found each Council I worked with using this system to be very knowledgeable and generous when it came time for the annual performance evaluation because they had a detailed accounting of what had been accomplished. It was easy for them to explain a pay raise and justify it to their constituency.

The second example is the Annual Plan of Work. I'll explain later how this tied into the rest of the city's management system. For now, let me just say that each year, along with adoption of the annual budget, I required each department to give me a relatively detailed plan of work which contained tasks, performance measures, and timelines. When combined across all departments, we had thousands of tasks to manage. I had an administrative person in my office log each task and its' associated deadline into a database. That person would follow the database throughout the year and tell the Department Head and me if a performance benchmark had been missed. Conditions changed throughout the year and plans occasionally had to be adjusted. We had an approval process for that as well. Again, it was a very accountable system. Because of the accountability, things got done. Subordinate leaders felt comfortable with it because they created the plan and the timeline, with my approval. They were very clear about what was expected of them.

Moral Compass

I have already said a lot about the ethics and character required to be a good leader. Their importance cannot be over-stated and are worth repeating. These characteristics are not only a prerequisite for being a good leader, but they are also part of what a leader does. Leaders promote, by clarity and example, the ethics and behavioral standards of the organization; they enforce those standards upon the organization. They are the moral compass of the entire management structure. In the public sector, and arguably in the private sector as well, it isn't just what you do that counts, but also how you do it. The ends do not always justify the means. The leader at the top of the organization chart must have and promote a moral compass that ensures the work is being done in both ethical and moral ways.

I had a colleague in a neighboring jurisdiction who served as its Administrator. Jurisdiction to jurisdiction, we worked well together. I respected her long list of accomplishments and her long tenure. One day I was surprised to learn that she had resigned her position, as had her husband who also worked for that same organization. Accompanying the resignations were rumored questions regarding nepotism, mishandling of raises and retirement accounts. No formal accusations had been made; no criminal charges had been filed, just questions being asked. The questions alone were enough to taint her moral authority, hamper her ability to lead the organization and bring an end to a long, and otherwise distinguished, career in public service.

The moral compass must always point true north; even the appearance of impropriety must be avoided.

Helping People

While it is true that leaders get things done through other people, good leaders don't mistreat people by using their skills and abilities to advance the goals of the organization without regard for the needs of the people doing the work. They are genuinely helpful to those people. Good leaders build and strengthen people. At the end of the day, leadership is entirely a people-oriented business that should help build people up.

So, how does one go about being helpful to people in the workplace? How does one build and strengthen people? Obviously, the first step is to genuinely care about the people you work with in equal measure to your concern for the mission of the organization. This may be counter-intuitive to those who have been trained, as I was, to think only of the good of the organization, or to only focus on getting the job done. Good leaders must learn to focus on the needs of their people as well as the needs of their organization. Both are important. A simple sincere question can go a long way, "How can I help you do your job?"

If you care about people, you will want them to succeed and become the best they can be. Although not always easy to do effectively, honest feedback is one of the greatest gifts, and greatest helps, a leader can give to a follower. Talking about expectations before an assignment, coaching along the way, and following up with an after-action review can be very helpful to the advancement of subordinates because it provides opportunity for feedback. There is a lesson in here for followers as well. Even when leaders want to be helpful and are willing to give feedback, it is not always easy to do; followers should be receptive. Feedback should be sought by followers. A wise person will ask the boss or mentor for feedback and coaching and then receive it without resistance or excuses or justifications. Take it constructively and be grateful for it. Honest feedback is one of the greatest gifts that can be given. It brings light into personal blind spots. It is also one of the easiest gifts to withhold. When it is withheld, the follower doesn't even know what has been missed. Resistance of any kind encourages mentors to withhold wisdom. Resistant followers may think they are doing well because they haven't received negative feedback, but they have missed out on gaining something positive that would have helped their career greatly.

I recall a Police Chief I worked with. He had worked in the Police Department for several years when I asked him if he would serve as Chief. He initially declined because he humbly thought that a better Chief could be found. I disagreed and invited him on several more occasions. Finally, after some family input and my assurance that he could return to his former position if being Chief didn't work out, he decided to take the job. On a regular basis, he and I would go for a ride in his unmarked car. Invariably, he would ask me, "How am I doing, boss?" "Is there anything I'm doing that's causing you a problem?" "Is there anything that I can do better?" "What do you need from me that you're not getting?" The rides also provided an opportunity for me to ask him similar questions. He made my job easier, and he helped me be a better City Manager. He treated his subordinates in a similar manner. In my view, he was a great Police Chief and a great leader.

Training is another area where leaders can help their people. Cities, generally, and City Managers specifically, get so caught up in their daily work that they forget to take time to rejuvenate and learn. Leaders need to make sure their people take time to learn new things and to get a variety of training. Yes, it is costly. Yes, it takes precious time. Yes, it is vital to the growth of people.

Another way to be helpful and to grow people is to give them special assignments in areas that will tax the skills that they need to develop. These assignments will be challenging, and they will provide opportunity for feedback and for learning through experience.

There is a fear among some leaders that if they grow and develop their subordinate leaders, they will lose them, that they will go find other jobs for more money in other organizations. My advice: get over it. While it may even be true that they will leave for greater opportunity, I can think of no greater compliment than to have been a mentor that helped develop great people. Consider the other side of the coin; if you don't help your people to develop, your own organization will become mediocre. It will be difficult to attract people with great potential into the organization.

When I was once being interviewed as a finalist for a City Manager position, I was asked a question intended to measure my understanding of the role of leadership and to help the decision-makers better understand my leadership style. The question was, "If the city were a football team, what position would you play?" I found out later how other finalists answered that question. One said cheerleader. Another said quarterback. Both were worthy and revealing answers. My answer: coach.

Being helpful to people, in my view, is the best way to lead and a critical component of what leaders do.

In Summary, How to Lead a City

This chapter has discussed the first duty of a City Manager, which is Leadership. A City Manager, by definition, is out in front of the city organization. Whether or not City Managers are effective in their leadership will depend on how well they command the respect of followers through moral authority, are driven by the right core values, have a vision for what needs to be done, are crystal clear about the mission, set a worthy example, and are able to motivate followers to action.

Getting the job done makes a City Manager effective but there is a difference between effective leadership and good leadership. Good leadership requires a leader to be ethical. Good leadership values honesty, fairness, the truth, keeping your word, and integrity. Good leadership values people because, at the end of the day, leadership is a people business.

Good, effective leaders have several characteristics in common. Among those characteristics are being intelligent, confident, trustworthy, communicative, approachable, predictable, steady, responsible, courageous, bold, and being good decision-makers.

Exercising leadership requires leaders to do certain things. Among those things are to cast a vision for what the organization can become, provide clarity on issues and methods, define the mission and expectations of the organization, model acceptable behavior, be motivational, be accountable, and provide a moral compass for the organization.

The best leaders are helpful to their followers. City Managers are hired by City Councils to get the job done, to ensure that the "ends" of the organization are achieved. But it doesn't stop there. The "means" by which things get done are critically important as well. Consequently, leaders that put the interests of their followers at the top of their priority list, that develop the talents and abilities of their subordinates, that provide opportunity and growth to the people they work with, also employ the best means in the process of achieving the ends of the organization. City Managers that teach, coach, and develop their followers become the very best leaders.

Now, it's time to move on to the second duty of a City Manager, Advising the City Council.

ADVISING
the City Council

Advising the City Council

The City Manager's Second Duty

While it is true that City Managers are the employees of the City Council, it is also true that they are advisers to the City Council. Most City Charters, or other governing laws, prescribe the duties of the City Managers and require them to advise the City Council of the financial and other operational conditions of the city. Common charter language often reads something like this: "Keep the Council advised of the financial condition and future needs of the city and make such recommendations as may seem to him desirable." Those same charters, de facto, define the governing team as being comprised of the City Council, the Mayor, and the City Manager. They require the City Manager to attend all meetings of the City Council; they give the City Manager the right and obligation to speak at those meetings, but without the right to vote. City Managers play a vital role in advising and coaching their City Councils in their proper role as elected officials.

Timidly inclined City Managers may find this concept a little surprising and, perhaps, uncomfortable because they view their job as only doing what the City Council tells them to do; they wait for the Council to give direction, then carry it out with efficiency and effectiveness. This view, however falls short of city management excellence and fails to recognize this second major duty of the City Manager. It also assumes that City Councils understand their duty and are expert in carrying it out. It is an assumption that should not be made before proving it to be true.

In terms of governing the city, it is my contention that the most knowledgeable and the most experienced person on the governing team should be the City Manager. If not, the City Council has selected the wrong person for that job. This does not mean that the City Council becomes a puppet of the City Manager. It does not mean that the City

Manager secretly runs the city from a safe, but hidden, perch. On the contrary, it means that the City Manager clearly 1) understands the duties of both the City Manager's office and the City Council and 2) assists the Council in performing their duties to govern the city. The best City Managers have only the highest of respect for their bosses and the governing roles they play. They know that there are certain vital functions that only the City Council can do; they know the difference between City Council and City Manager duties and they know how to help the City Council fulfill their unique duty. This is done by helping them to understand their job; ensuring they understand all the issues and best practices, all the alternatives, all the costs and impacts of their decisions. City Managers will assist without substituting their own values for those of the City Council and without attempting to persuade the Council to a specific result. The City Council is elected to make value judgements and to set governing policy; the City Manager is not. The second duty of a City Manager is to advise the City Council professionally, independently, neutrally, and wisely.

What is an advisor?

An advisor is one who informs, cautions, warns, coaches and recommends. In the case of city management, the advisor is not the decision-maker. Due deference needs to be given to this point without shrinking from the responsibility to advise. The greatest respect a City Manager can show to the City Council is to help them do their duty in the most professional way possible and then to let them do it.

The way the advice is given will make a great deal of difference in whether the advice is accepted. There will be times when the Council, or members thereof, do not want honest and candid advice. They will want to hear only what they already believe. They will want the City Manager to reinforce what they already want to do. Speaking truth to power is always a challenge. A City Manager must truthfully tell the City Council what they need to hear and not just what they may want to hear.

I recall an instance I observed before becoming a City Manager. A City Council member was very concerned with underage youth drinking and driving. His solution was to prohibit single can sales of beer at convenience stores. He came into a Council workshop one evening and made his proposal. He had previously "greased the skids" with two of his fellow Council members so that, when he proposed it, the Council was ready to receive a motion and vote. In their own minds they had properly defined the problem and selected the best alternative to solve it; they were not open to further discussion. They wanted what they wanted, and they wanted it right now. They voted on it and approved the proposal. The city got belated push back from retailers and citizens alike, along with national attention for being the only city in the country that promoted impaired driving by requiring consumers to buy an entire six-pack rather than a single can. It was an issue where an advisor could have saved the city some embarrassment.

Another interesting example occurred in a city that had been receiving evacuees from a hurricane event. It had been going on for several days and it was taxing the resources of the city. One of the City Council members suggested that an idle retirement home be activated to make it suitable for evacuees. The cost of readying the facility was high, the time it would take was significant, and the peak of the event had passed. The idea should have been scrubbed much more than it was. But because "the Council" wanted it, even without formal Council vote, the City Manager quickly moved forward with it. Compared to the cost and effort of readying the facility, its usefulness was predictably marginal; It was another issue that could have used better advising.

To the detriment of the cities in both examples, the management team failed in its duty to professionally advise. The intentions were not sinister but in the absence of understanding the duty to advise, politics trumped good decisions and good policy-making.

Corpus Christi, Texas, was facing a huge problem with deferred maintenance on its street system. The cost of getting the existing street system back in reasonable shape was estimated at $1 billion. The city had previously considered, and then declined, enacting a street maintenance fee to offset some of that cost. The fee issue came up again while I was there. We responded to it by using the 3-D process: Discover, Debate, then Decide. I will discuss this process in more detail later in this chapter. For over a year, the item was under discovery. Every week the staff would bring facts regarding the street system before the City Council. Council would study the material, ask questions, and consider alternatives. It was a very public process. Everyone learned a lot and the Council received much input from citizens. After about a year or so, people began to press the Council for a decision because it had been fully vetted and there were no more valid questions that could be asked, no more opinions that could be heard. The Council and the people were fully informed. When it finally came to a vote, it passed unanimously. There were no lawsuits following the action, as some had expected. The City Council had been fully advised on a controversial and very important issue.

This case study is a good example of how to make effective, transparent decisions. It is a good example of how to advise the City Council by ensuring that they know the issue, know the alternatives, and know the costs and the impacts of their decision. The process of advising the City Council in this manner takes more energy and time but it yields better results.

To be a valuable advisor to the City Council, the City Manager must be trusted. To be trusted, one must be believed. To be believed, one must tell the truth, the whole truth and nothing but the truth. It goes back to leadership and ethics.

Implied in this whole process of advising the City Council is the fact that City Managers must know, not only their own role and business, but the role and business of the City Council as well. This is a key point and one that will need further clarification.

What do City Councils Actually do?

Before City Managers can effectively advise their City Councils, they must first clearly understand what a City Council is supposed to do. While that statement makes sense, many City Managers fail to have a precise understanding of the role of their City Council. Being clear about the Council's purpose and responsibilities helps prevent "mission creep." Mission creep occurs when the role, purpose, or mission continues to expand beyond what was originally intended. Usually, this happens one little logical increment at a time until we arrive at a place that no one originally intended to be. Being very clear about what is supposed to be done, and staying razor focused on it is vital to good governance. A City Council governs through five basic responsibilities. They are to:

- Provide leadership.
- Approve high level goals and change targets.
- Set governing policy.
- Provide oversight, and
- Perform required ministerial acts.

Before this chapter is concluded, I will cover each of these five City Council duties in more detail.

Of equal importance is for City Managers to understand what City Council members do not do. <u>City Councils</u>, as a body or as individuals, <u>do not</u>:

- Manage the daily operations of the city. Their policy, however, may outline boundaries within which the City Manager's management decisions may be made.
- Direct the appointment or removal of subordinates of the City Manager; provided that in some City Charters, they are required to give advice and consent to certain personnel actions.

- Give, or imply, orders to subordinates of the City Manager.

By comparing the roles and responsibilities of City Managers and City Councils, one can quickly see that, while they are intimately related, they are completely different and separate from each other. It is vital to understand that they are complimentary and not competitive. While they may encourage, coach and advise, City Managers cannot do the work of elected officials. Likewise, City Councils cannot, and should not try to, perform the duties of the City Manager. If a City Manager is not performing, the Council should replace her, not attempt to compensate for inadequate performance by doing her duties for her. Cities function well only when both parties are doing their unique responsibilities, working in partnership to accomplish everything that is required to fulfill a city's mission.

One soundbite explanation of the role of Managers and Councils is this: Councils make policy and Managers carry out policy. While that statement is true on its face, it is over simplified. Carrying out policy is only one of the duties of City Managers and making policy is only one of the duties of City Councils. Failing to understand and act on the full complement of duties leads to malperformance on the part of both City Managers and City Councils.

Why is serving on a City Council so difficult?

In most cases, people run for City Council offices to serve the community and make what they perceive to be important changes. Many times, candidates run for office to correct single issues, such as a zoning or financial issue or a law enforcement grievance. Once elected, they quickly find that the work they were just elected to do is very hard and much more complicated than they first imagined. The number of times a newly elected Councilmember has approached me to admit the overwhelming size and complexity of the new job are too numerous to count. I have found that the learning curve for newly elected officials is typically one to two years, which is much longer than most initially imagined.

For many City Councilmembers, being placed in front of the world to be voted on is, by itself, an exercise in torture. Then, after being elected, doing the job is, as I have said, very difficult. There are many reasons for the difficulty. The following are several of them:

Complexity

I have seen it a thousand times. When facing a difficult decision, citizens will come into a Council meeting and say, with much tone in their voice, "Why don't you just do so and so?" as if that solution were the most obvious and common-sense solution available and we are all idiots for not thinking of it already. City Councils and city Staff are not idiots. Difficult problems do not have easy solutions. If they did, they wouldn't be difficult problems; they would be easy problems. And, they would have been solved long before they become discussion topics in the public arena. All hard decisions are complex. They have technical, financial, legal and political implications that prevent simple answers.

Costs

Every decision carries a price tag. The price is always higher than we want it to be, always. That is the world we live in simply because of the cost of goods and services. That statement is even more true in the public sector because there are so many legal requirements that must be met to guarantee transparency, equal treatment, non-discrimination, best value and lowest cost. Another complicating factor in the public sector is that people tend to think that someone else should pay the price. Higher governments shift the cost burden to lower governments through unfunded mandates and tax exemptions. city governments shift costs through deferred maintenance, underfunding retirement, under compensating employees, playing games with interfund charges, unwise borrowing, impact fees and service fees. Sometimes the shifting more accurately places the cost burden where it properly belongs; sometimes it just creates new problems to solve. For the most part, this all happens because people fail, or refuse, to recognize how expensive things really are and that there is a price tag to be paid for every decision made.

Non-partisan, but political

In nearly every city, the Charter or State Law requires City Councils to be non-partisan. In other words, they do not run on a party ticket or otherwise identify themselves with a political party. In today's divided society, however, it would be naïve to think that party politics did not play a role in any election. Even beyond the influence of party politics, there are the honest differences of opinion about what's most or least important, what needs to change and what needs to stay the same. There is the influence of personal ambition of the individual council members and the very real impact of influential special interests. One definition of politics deals with the balance between conflict and compromise. For many newly elected City Council members, it takes a while to understand that they cannot get anything done without the agreement of a majority of the City Council. Their ability to get anything done comes down to the value and effectiveness of their relationship with their colleagues on the City Council. This is one of the reasons why some individual Councilmembers begin to interfere in the City Manager's duties. They can't get the City Council to agree with them, so they attempt to bully their way through the staff. Serving on a City Council is a team sport and, while City Councils may be non-partisan, they are political in the sense of Council member relationships with each other.

Unrealistic expectations

It has been said that people can hate the Congress and love their congressman. That is obviously a true saying when we look at the low approval ratings of the Congress and see people getting repeatedly re-elected. In my view, this is a failing of the electorate who have unrealistic expectations of their elected representatives. This same attitude and problem bleeds over into city government. Electors get frustrated with things they don't agree with or understand. Then, they elect someone to go "shake things up," which only causes more frustration and unmet expectation because no one has clarified what those expectations ought to be. The problem continues to grow, causing mistrust and dissatisfaction. It's a circular problem.

Newly elected City Council members have the hill of unrealistic expectations to climb before they ever start their public service. Being able to exceed expectations is the very definition and measuring stick of excellent service. When expectations are not clearly defined and agreed upon, people create their own definition. This lack of clarity and lack of agreement make it impossible to meet or exceed expectations, therefore making it very difficult to be successful on a City Council. It's a tough gig.

Lack of Professional Support

I hate to admit it but, in a few cities, another thing that makes serving and being successful on a City Council very difficult is a lack of professional support from the City Manager and staff. If the necessary partnership between the City Manager and the City Council is broken because the City Manager does not understand or fulfill his roles and responsibilities, immeasurable damage to the organization can be caused. Too often I have seen City Managers improperly or incompletely define their role. They don't recognize or perform all their vital duties. They don't help the City Council carry out their unique and vital role. Unknowingly some City Councils think it is wonderful that they have a City Manager who is willing to do whatever whim may come into the Council's minds or fulfill every wish of their heart, neither party realizing what tremendous downstream damage that may cause.

So, getting elected to and serving on a City Council is hard work. Once elected, there are duties that must be performed and there are some things that should not be done. For City Managers to properly fulfill their duty to advise the City Council, they must first clearly understand what City Councils do. Let's move on to talk about how to advise and coach the boss.

How to advise the City Council

There is a difference between giving advice and making a recommendation. Recommendations occur all the time on routine matters, paying bills, approving ministerial actions, and approving actions that clearly fall within approved policy. Recommendations occur on repetitive issues and signify that staff has done routine due diligence on behalf of the Council to ensure compliance with previously approved policy.

Advice occurs when the Council is working its way through new, unique and difficult issues for which there is no previously approved policy. It occurs on issues that require the discovery of new facts, identification of alternatives and costs and the articulation of new policy. Advice occurs in the creation of new policy; recommendations occur in the application of old policy.

When advising the City Council, the mission of the City Manager is not to persuade. It is to inform by helping the Council discover the facts and arrive at their own value-laden decisions.

This is going to sound too simple, like a "Duh," and it is simple but it's not easy: Always advise the City Council with candor and honesty. Because they are dealing with value-laden decisions, individually or collectively, the Council will not always want to hear all the facts. Give all the facts to the Council anyway. I'm not saying to be rude or insensitive or politically naïve; I am saying just give them all the facts and tell them the whole truth. They may sometimes think you're being political or taking sides or substituting personal values for theirs. Don't deviate from your truthful neutrality. Practice no deception by omission or by intent. The foundation of trust is the truth; without the truth, there is no trust. If there is no trust, there is no strong relationship; there is no progress; and, in the end, there is no job for the City Manager.

Base your advice on the facts and the best professional interpretation of what those facts will lead to. Do not base advice on personal, value-laden opinions about what should be done with the facts or about which alternative should be selected. In fact, on the most unique and difficult issues, be hesitant to give an opinion at all. As a City Manager, be very clear regarding the difference between advising and recommending.

To obtain and understand the facts, be analytical. If you are not analytical, have someone close to you who can be analytical. If the facts are well gathered and well interpreted, they will tell the story that the Council needs to hear to make their own good decisions. Be very transparent about the whole process. When there is room for reasonable alternative interpretations or alternative solutions, be honest about that as well. Remember, the job is to inform, not to persuade. I can recall many times, when City Councils have been wrestling with difficult issues, they would prematurely ask me what my recommendation was. It was too early for a recommendation because they had not created policy; they had not done their job. I understood the difference between their job and my job; it was my job to help them do their job and insist that they do it. The biggest service I could do them was to ensure that they do what only they can do, make the difficult, value-laden decisions. When they prematurely asked for a recommendation, they were desperate for a shortcut through the very difficult policy-making or decision-making process. They trusted me; they trusted my opinions. Because the decision was not mine to make, I would withhold my opinion and say something like, "I have given you the best information about the facts that I can; I have given you the alternatives; I have given you the costs to those alternatives. The decision must be yours." Occasionally someone would press me beyond that response. In that case, if they had struggled long enough with the issue, I may have said something like, "If the decision were mine to make, I would do so and so, but the decision is not mine to make." In most cases, that language would jolt them back to understanding that the hard decision was theirs alone to make, and then they would make it. Regardless of their ultimate decision, I would feel like I had done my job and was satisfied that they had done theirs.

The duty to advise includes 1) treating all members of the Council equally, 2) ensuring they have all the pertinent information, 3) making sure all questions are answered and all opinions, even difficult opposing ones, are heard before they vote.

It took decades for me to figure this stuff out so don't breeze over it without giving it due consideration.

Let me recommend a process which we clarified and used in Corpus Christi as the City Council worked through the difficult issue of considering whether to establish a street fee. We ended up calling it the Three D process. The process includes three steps:

- <u>Discover.</u> Clearly define the problem. Completely understand it. Unearth the facts. Identify all the viewpoints. Clarify all the alternatives and costs. Answer all the questions asked by the Council. Take as many meetings as necessary to accomplish this.
- <u>Debate.</u> Following the discovery phase, the Council debates, discusses, invites input, and hears all opinions about the topic, from themselves and the public.
- <u>Decide.</u> Only after completing the first two steps is a decision considered. The direction is ultimately set by majority vote of the whole Council. My experience is, after this process, most votes are unanimous because everyone understands the problem; everyone has had their say; reasonable compromises have occurred, and the Council has created their own consensus.

The process of advising in this manner takes time and must be done in order. Think of it like, Ready, Aim, Fire. Fire, Ready, Aim, simply does not yield the same result! If the City Council fails to do one of the steps or if they get the steps out of order, it doesn't go well.

Caution: All too often I have seen Councilmembers, staff or members of the public who just want to get on with it. The process seems slow or unnecessary to them. They make their mind up early and turn their efforts from discovery to persuasion. If there are any questions still unanswered, the process isn't over and it's not time to decide yet.

Again, take the street fee in Corpus Christi as an example. That issue had been brought, unsuccessfully, before the City Council many times, for many years, before we used this process. It took over a year of discovery and debate, but resulted in the Council making a well-informed, value-driven decision that they were all fully committed to.

Further, a City Manager needs to understand that problems look different depending on one's perspective. Staff tend to see neighborhood issues from a point of view that asks, "How can we uphold our policy and give the biggest benefit to the most people for the least cost?" Many elected officials tend to look at the same issue and ask, "How can we strengthen our community by bringing opposing viewpoints together, even if it costs a little more or if we need to be a little less efficient or a little less consistent with previous policy?" Both perspectives are necessary. The City Manager must understand them both and help the different perspectives understand each other.[1]

Working with and advising a City Council requires a good understanding of human nature. It takes a healthy self-image and a lot of courage to run for public office. In fact, I have heard some people say that all politicians are egomaniacs. While that is certainly an overstatement, generally, they do have healthy egos to manage. Some City Managers have more ego than true self-confidence. If all those egos go unchecked, there are going to be problems. A little

---

[1] For informative reading regarding the relationship between local government administration and politics, I recommend the publications of Dr John Nalbandian.

humility and a lot of professional understanding go a long way in advising the City Council.

It has been said that the boss is not always right, but he is always the boss. Good employment etiquette and plain common sense requires that a City Manager always respect the City Council and treat them with professional courtesy, even when they decide something the City Manager thinks is less than optimal. It's the right thing to do. Absent that, efforts to advise the City Council will be ineffective. I recall an instance when we were working through a Financial Governing Policy. The question was what size of reserve should we target for the General Fund. All the facts and my best judgement pointed to a 25% reserve. The Council decided on an 18% reserve. It was a split decision. The minority of Council wanted me to object and make a big deal out of it. The Council had all the facts; they had the alternatives; and in this case, they had debated it at length. From my perspective, the Council, by majority vote, had spoken; their decision needed to be honored. And it was.

A City Manager needs to be comfortable in the role of teacher and coach, to both the staff and to the City Council. If the City Manager does not have superior grasp of how city government works or how a plethora of management techniques and styles apply or if he does not understand the role and responsibility of the City Manager in comparison to that of the City Council, he is probably not ready to fulfill his role as Chief Advisor to the City Council.

So, advising the City Council is much more than making recommendations or telling them what to do. It is teaching, coaching, and leading them through a process so they can effectively tell you what to do, so they can rightly fulfill their responsibility to govern the city.

Let's move on to address how a City Manager can assist and advise the City Council in their leadership duties.

Advising the City Council regarding Their Leadership Responsibilities

Leadership is the City Council's first and most basic responsibility. A City Manager must clearly understand both leadership and the City Council's role in leadership to properly advise them. In a previous section of this book, I talked about leadership. In that part of the book, I expressed thoughts on what leadership is, how to distinguish good from bad leadership, the key characteristics of leaders and what leaders do. All those thoughts apply to City Council Leadership as well, and perhaps even more so, because, while not always shown on the organization chart, the City Council is at the top of the municipal enterprise and superior to the City Manager. Beyond that, I will now address some specific leadership issues that affect elected City Council members.

Advising the City Council Regarding Leadership Inside of the City Council

The first and most obvious area of leadership for Council members is leadership within the council itself. City Councils are comprised of an odd number of voting members. Each of those individual members has a leadership role to play, but the Council can accomplish nothing individually. They can only get things done when they act as a body. The reason for the odd number is so that they cannot have a tie when they vote. There will always be a majority to move the Council in a direction. However, no one should be fooled by a majority vote. A simple majority may work in the National Congress (or not), but, in a city, it signifies a very weak City Council. The relationships become frayed. They become divided. Their decisions do not hold; they are reversed at the first opportunity. The Council becomes unpredictable and unreliable. Instead, they should be seeking a solid consensus, and that takes leadership. Seeking a consensus doesn't mean that each member needs to surrender his values or agree with every other member on every subject that comes before them. It does mean that an individual Council member's ultimate effectiveness will depend on how well she works with the group; how well she can influence others to act and how well she can apply leadership principles. Unless the Councilmembers can exercise the leadership characteristics and skills previously described, those Council members will be ineffective. The City Manager must advise and assist them to be true to themselves while they become good leaders within the City Council.

Given the current state of American politics and recognizing that much of the reputation of national politics will naturally bleed over onto local politics, no one should be surprised to see ineffective leadership in any elected body. No one should be surprised to see elected officials falsely advertising their role in that ineffective process as being heroic and noble while the other guys are just a bunch of slugs. We, however, should not be fooled by the rhetoric. We should recognize it for what it is: ineffective leadership. The opposite is also true. We should recognize and reward successful leadership when it occurs. I'm not just talking about local elected officials, I'm talking about all elected officials who get things done through solid consensus, in the right way. Elected officials are not the only ones who should understand leadership and be accountable for exercising it; the electorate has a responsibility to good leadership as well. To select good leaders and hold them accountable, we must be good leaders ourselves.

I have seen it too many times. Constituents will criticize elected officials for agreeing with each other too much. If there are not dissenting votes, they will accuse Council members of being rubber stamps, of surrendering their values and campaign promises or of not properly doing their homework. They will unknowingly intimidate their elected officials into poor leadership practices. When properly functioning, disagreements on Council should be rare occasions. Contrary to standard political practice, we should insist that elected Council members cooperate with each other and work together, find acceptable compromises to their differences and find the win-win, rather than insisting that they disagree with each other and work from a win-lose perspective.

The City Manager's duty is to help the City Council to exercise good, effective leadership inside of the Council itself.

In my career, I have faced some big challenges regarding City Council leadership. When I arrived in one particular city, it was standard practice for the Council to make its decisions on a thin majority vote. Relationships were, indeed, frayed. Sides had been taken. There had been arguments and physical confrontations. There were pending personal lawsuits. There were rumors that Councilmembers were carrying concealed weapons in the Council meetings, not for protection against terrorists but for protection from each other. They were a tough Council and it was a serious test of the principles I am espousing in this book, but they worked.

Advising the City Council Regarding Leadership with Their Constituency

The $64,000 question, a reference to a 1950's TV game show, is this: Is an elected official in office to do what their constituency wants them to do or to do what they think is right? This assumes that the constituency can speak with one voice, which, of course, they cannot. There is always a difference between what the elected official thinks and what at least a part of the constituency thinks. It further assumes that the constituency has the same facts and understanding as their elected official, which, in most cases, they do not. Another way to phrase the question is, are elected officials there to lead or be led?

The obvious answer, from my perspective, is that they are there to lead. This means that, not only must they interact with and listen to their constituency, but they must also explain; they must inform and motivate their constituency. They must have the courage to occasionally disagree with some of their constituency. They must do the right thing. They must lead.

Keep in mind that the American federal system of government is a Republic, not a Democracy. In other words, we elect people to represent us and to vote on the issues in our behalf; we do not vote directly on the issues. For example, we do not vote on the national appropriations bill or the national debt ceiling; our representative in Congress does that for us. When they vote, some of the constituency will agree with the vote, and some will not. When we vote for the President, we are not voting directly for the President, we are voting to give direction to a portion of the Electoral College from our state. It is the Electoral College that votes for the President. We are a Republic, not a Democracy. City government is no different. We elect City Council members to vote on the issues. It is only the rarest of issues (for example, initiative petitions, referendums and the issuance of general obligation debt) that city voters get to vote directly on an issue. We expect that those whom we elect will become informed on the details and make the best decisions possible. We expect them to make decisions that are in our best interest. Therein comes the rub: people can see the same issue in different ways. We are constantly judging our elected officials on their decisions by what we think and what we think we know about the issues. Few of us are as well informed as our elected representatives. None of us see the same problem in totally the same way. We need to be more tolerant and understanding of the difficulty our representatives face. Having said that, I believe elected officials need to a better job of truly leading and building consensus among their constituents. Constituents need to do a better job of trusting them. If constituents can't trust them, they need to get involved earlier in the process to recruit trustworthy people to run for public office.

To illustrate these points, I am recalling an experience I had early in my career as a City Manager. At the time I served there, my city was the fastest growing city in the United States with a population under 50,000. Because of the growth, the infrastructure demands were enormous. The Council desperately wanted to address those growing infrastructure requirements. An additional amount of property tax was proposed; it was to be dedicated to infrastructure. At the request of Council, it was placed into the annual budget. Public hearings were required to pass the budget and approve the tax rate. I considered the Council to be very courageous and forward thinking to take such action. The Council was unanimous in their direction. Of course, word of the tax increase spread throughout the community by normal and informal means. As the time of the hearing approached, it became apparent that the City Hall would not be large enough to accommodate the number of people expected to attend. Arrangements were made to move the hearing to the local junior high school where the auditorium would accommodate many hundreds of people. For city officials, it was an ugly, angry meeting. The auditorium was filled. As the meeting got ready to start, people were chanting slogans and waving signs in protest of the tax increase. As the meeting progressed, scores of people spoke against the proposal. Only one, who happened to serve on the city's Planning Commission, spoke in favor of it. As was allowed in those days, the Council temporarily recessed the meeting and retired to a back room to deliberate on what they had heard. Four of the five members still believed the tax increase to be necessary and wanted to move forward. The Mayor, while still believing the tax increase to be necessary, was unwilling to move forward if the people didn't want it. When they asked me what I thought, I told them that the decision was, of course, theirs to make but I predicted there would be consequences. I asked them if they were prepared for the consequences. They were. They reconvened the meeting and announced their decision. They would move forward with approving the budget, including the tax increase. It was an unpopular decision, to say the least.

The next day, the Mayor resigned. Within the next year or so, two of the Councilmembers left the city. One moved to a neighboring community. Another moved out of state. A third member decided to not run for re-election. There were significant changes on the City Council and turmoil inside of City Hall. In December following the next election, I had a favorable performance review with the new City Council and they gave me a raise for good performance. I thought I had survived the turmoil but, by March, they were asking for my resignation.

If I could go back in time, I would do things differently. For one thing, I would be much more engaged in advising and coaching the City Council. Even though I thought I was the bee's knees, I was young and inexperienced for this type of intense decision-making. If I could go back in time, I would treat that tax increase in the same way we treated the street fee in Corpus Christi. I would do everything in my power to advise them to go through a 3-D process: Discover, Debate, and then Decide. I would advise the Council to exercise strong and effective leadership by publicly talking about the issue until everyone got sick of talking about it and begged for a decision. If I could go back in time, we would have never had the giant public hearing in the junior high school because we would have thoroughly and transparently dealt with the problem before it ever made its way into the city budget. If the constituency had understood the problem as well as the City Council, I believe they would have responded differently. Hard experience has taught me many lessons. This was one of them.

Every elected City Council member must decide what his proper role is in relation to his constituency. Will they lead or will they be led? Are they willing to do the hard work of leadership or will they do the easier work of rhetoric? The electorate needs to understand the political process and have realistic expectations of their elected officials. The City Manager plays a pivotal role in advising and supporting the City Council in their constituent leadership duties.

Advising the City Council Regarding Leadership in the Community

For City Council members, leadership in the community is different than the leadership with their constituency. Leadership with the constituency includes educating and informing people about the specific issues, while leadership in the community involves representing and supporting the City Council to the public.

By virtue of being elected, City Council members are no longer just private citizens; they are representatives of the city and they are public figures. Their actions and opinions become bigger than they were before they were elected. This can be very ego-reinforcing. However, once elected, City Council members have a duty to represent the City Council, as well as their own opinions. Because they campaign as individuals, and generally campaign on a platform of change, once elected, it is hard for many City Council members to understand that they are part of the very team they were criticizing on the campaign trail. All of my experience reinforces my opinion that when the public looks at the city, they do not see individuals; they see "the City." If there are problems, the public generally sees the City Council; they do not see Councilmember A or Councilmember B. On a national level, the phenomenon of hating the Congress and loving the Congressman holds true. The US Congress is composed of 535 people and a typical City Council is composed of less than nine. That phenomenon does not work on a local level. Council members too often act like it does, but it doesn't. In both formal and informal ways, City Council members will be asked for their insights and thoughts about city issues. It is wise for them to remember that they are part of the team. They should honestly speak for the team in positive ways, as well as for themselves. To maintain Council unity on issues still in progress, it is well for the Council to designate a single spokesperson until the issue is resolved so that the public is not getting multiple contradictory opinions before the issue is fully vetted. It just makes the Council look inept and weakens public confidence when that happens. Another negative impact of Councilmembers giving premature public comment is that it tends to force them into immovable positions before the full debate is concluded. Councilmembers need to remain open to learning and changing while the discovery and debate portions of the decision-making process are still on-going; otherwise, how will all the other Councilmembers have the opportunity to exercise their leadership responsibility to influence and motivate?

Note: With modern technology such as live streaming of meetings, PEG cable TV channels, website meeting archives and the news media, the public has full opportunity to see for themselves what the issues are and how the City Council is dealing with them. All that places a responsibility on the individual citizen to stay informed; it is transparent and it is a good thing.

The sanctity of majority rule is critical to the success of government at every level, including the city level. If that principle breaks down, government cannot be successful. Even if a Councilmember is on the minority side of the vote, once an issue is resolved the individuals should remember that they are still part of the team and support the decision. If they cannot support it, they should at least remain silent. The team will be dealing with more issues in the future. If they professionally disagree on an issue, that's one thing. If they trash the decision of the majority in a negative, political way, they will harm the integrity of the entire Council process. Because they are part of the Council, they will be harming themselves by poisoning future actions they may support. Let's back up a moment. Dissent on an issue is not a bad thing if the proper decision-making process has been followed (the Three-D process) if there has been full disclosure of facts and alternatives and if everyone has had their full say. By that time, the public will have had plenty of opportunity to understand and know what's going on. The biggest problems occur when issues are rammed through. Again, this comes back to good leadership practice.

In several of my cities there was at least one Councilmember who regularly voted no on issues coming before the Council. Without doing due diligence on the issues, their safe political move, as they saw it, was to vote no. Then, on their Facebook pages and in their public actions, they would be very critical of the city and of the City Council. They were contrary and undermining. For sure, they each had a certain following of people who were, themselves, dissatisfied with… everything. I'm still not sure if they were leaders among their supporters or were being led by them. Mostly, they were alone on the City Council, so they rarely changed the outcome on any of the issues. Always, they were disruptive of good decision-making, and consistently exercised poor community leadership. As I said before, honest dissent can be very constructive to the Council's decision-making process and good internal relations can be maintained with it. But irresponsible dissent for political purposes is destructive to the Council process and undermines public confidence in the entire elected body.

While ceremonial duties are primarily the responsibility of the Mayor, Council members may also, from time to time, be asked to represent the city in ceremonial ways. This may include public appearances, parades, invitations to speak at service clubs or groups, etc. Council members need to take this responsibility seriously and to realize how much it means to the people. Their participation is appreciated, and their absence is noticed. Some Council members are better at this type of work than others, but they all need to realize that this is not an individual honor; it is a group honor. Governing a city is a team sport where the game can only be won by the actions of the team, not its individual players.

As City Managers do their work, they need to always remember that they work for the City Council, as a whole, and not as individuals. As these things occur in real time, they are not always crystal clear. City Managers need to be very cautious to avoid unknowingly assisting to fracture the Council by supporting individual Council members in inappropriate activities. To properly advise, City Managers need to be fully conversant with City Council leadership responsibilities to the community.

Advising the City Council Regarding Leadership with other Governments

City governments do not work in isolation. Every region in the United States has a Council of Governments (COG), composed of cities and counties, that coordinate regional planning, the use of federal highway money and other matters. So, participating in and leading inside of the COG is important. Unfunded mandates from State and Federal governments makes up a huge portion of the city budget. So, working with state legislatures is critical, and generally requires cities to work together to have the biggest positive impact possible. Calling upon the resources of neighboring cities for mutual aid during emergencies and disasters works best when relationships have been fostered well in advance of the need. All these examples, and many more, demonstrate the need for developing relationships and exercising leadership with other governments. Elected Council members play a vital role in this area because of the commonality they share with other elected representatives and because, in some cases, membership in the group is only available to elected officials.

Some people are critical of the city over money and time they spend on memberships and participation in national, state and regional associations. These activities are, in my view, vital to the city's ability to build relationships and foster cooperation with other governments. Elected officials should take full advantage of these opportunities and provide all the leadership they can within them. Not every Council member needs to participate in every organization or every event. These opportunities can be divided among the various Council members. Doing city business in this manner is more efficient but it requires the Council members to communicate with each other and to share what they have learned and what they have done.

I would be less than candid if I did not admit that I have seen personal advantage taken of this responsibility by a few members of City Councils. I recall one of the Councils I worked with that seemed to view the annual National League of Cities conference in Washington DC to be as much of a personal vacation as a city duty. Additionally, I have worked with Councilmembers who were very good at hobnobbing with people from other governments. They used their relationships to benefit our city, even though their primary objective may have been to use those same relationships to aid them in seeking higher office in the future.

Despite the imperfections I have noted, Council leadership with other governments is vital to the good operation and well-being of a city. The City Manager needs to properly advise the City Council to ensure that it is done and done right.

We are ready to move away from advising on leadership and cover the next topic which deals with goals and change targets.

Advising the City Council Regarding Goals and Change Targets

Approving goals and change targets is the City Council's second basic responsibility. A City Manager must clearly understand this duty to be of assistance and be a good advisor to the City Council.

Let's get clarity on several important concepts. First, goals. What are goals? Goals are aspirations of some future state which is desirable to achieve. The best goals are well defined, achievable, and timebound.

The next concept to understand about goals in the city management arena is the idea of cascading goals. In other words, not all goals are equal, and some goals are nested inside higher goals. The City Council should concern itself only with the highest level of goals; they should be strategic in nature. For example, a goal to process a certain number of parking tickets during the year is an operational goal about which the Council should not be concerned. The goal to remain an agricultural community rather than to shift to a residential bedroom community is a strategic one with which the City Council must absolutely be involved. The highest level of goals is the strategic/governing type. These goals are primarily created by the management team and can only be approved by the City Council. The process of creating and approving this type of goal requires a process of total cooperation between City Council and City Manager. All other goals are nested inside of these goals. The next cascade are management goals. Management goals are nested inside of the parameters of strategic/governing goals; they are primarily created through the interplay between Department Heads and the City Manager; they are approved by the City Manager. The next cascade are operational goals. They are nested inside of the parameters of management goals; they are created through the interplay between Department Heads and their subordinate staff; they are approved by Department Heads.

Notice, I said that City Councils "approve" goals. Goalsetting is part of the planning process. Planning is a management function. City Councils should not be expected to perform the actual nitty gritty work of planning the goal. There is a cooperative interplay between the City Manager and the City Council so that, ultimately, the Council is satisfied with the strategic direction of the city. That direction will be approved, hopefully, by unanimous consensus, but, if not, by majority vote.

Many cities will set aside one or two days per year for a "strategic planning" session with the City Council. Often, the City Manager will act as facilitator. Sometimes, when a City Manager is not a skilled facilitator or when the Manager's active participation in the discussion is desired, a professional facilitator will be brought in to assist. The best I've seen those meetings produce is 1) a good teambuilding exercise and 2) a prioritized list of management goals. As often as not, those meetings have broken down into disagreements between Councilmembers about what operational detail is most important.

Admittedly, sometimes that's the best that can be done; I have never seen those meetings produce a truly strategic goal. I think producing strategic/governing goals is much harder work than a one-day planning session. It is far better for the City Manager to use his staff to do the nitty gritty hard work of planning and then get it onto the City Council's agenda and 3-D process it through to consensus approval. As a practical matter, it's the only way that hard work will get done. No offense is intended to the City Council at all; they simply do not have the time or the expertise to do this work. They absolutely do have the time to understand it after its done, amend it if necessary and approve it. More will be said about Management's responsibility to plan, and the process by which it is done, in the next chapter. The City Council should insist that the City Manager work that entire planning process, with appropriate check and approval points by the City Council.

Change Targets are like goals. They represent major shifts in emphasis or priority. In most cases, they can be expressed in the same language and handled in the same way as goals. An example: We want to defund the police department. If serious about that change target, a whole host of actions need to be taken to accomplish it. If serious about accomplishing the change target, the City Council should require the City Manager to bring them a plan containing a host of timebound, accountable goals and actions for their review, revision and approval.

Change and change management occurs throughout the city all the time. It is an on-going activity and one of the many skills that good managers need to develop. Mostly, those routine changes occur to align the city operations with routine operating goals. Major shifts in policy, and therefore city services, need to be approved by the City Council before being placed into action.

Advising the City Council Regarding Making Good Policy

If you were to ask any City Council member what her primary duty is, the answer would invariably be, "To make policy." However, if you were to follow that up with a couple more questions, the answers would not be as clear cut. For example, what is policy? Most would answer that the ordinances, resolutions and budgets they pass are their policies. While partly true, that would be an incomplete answer. For the City Manager's purposes, policy is a concisely explicit statement, selected from many alternatives, that gives predictable direction for both current and future actions. Ordinances, including the annual budget, are neither concise, clear or comprehensive enough to fulfill all the policy duties of City Council. Proper policies adopted by resolution could be. So, if you were to ask City Council to show you their book of policies, very few in the country, if any, could do it. Most cannot answer the basic questions; most do not understand the power or the importance of governing by policy; most have not created governing policy.[2]

Most cities have a financial policy of sorts because the Government Finance Officers Association (GFOA) requires the inclusion of financial policy statements in a city's Comprehensive Annual Financial Report for it to qualify for their certificate of excellence in financial reporting. Most cities of any size greatly desire to have this certification. This is the operational work primarily of the Finance Director and the City Council does not generally give it much more thought than to adopt the budget and approve receiving the Comprehensive Annual Financial Report.

Many cities will have outlined rules for managing their employees, something like a Human Resource Handbook or a Personnel Policies and Procedures Manual. Again, this is typically an operational policy book which may or may not be adopted by the City Council. To be accredited by a national association, the Police Department must first have a comprehensive set of operational policies. To get these policies in place, it typically takes about two years of dedicated work on the part of a specially designated team of police officers. The

---

[2] For informative reading regarding policy governance, I recommend the works of Dr John Carver.

accrediting agency evaluates the effectiveness of the policies and measures the departments performance against the policies before accrediting them. Again, these policies are operational and typically not approved by the City Council.

So, I'm not saying that cities don't have policies, because they do. I'm saying that most cities do not have <u>governing</u> policies. Most cities do not have their policies organized, structured and published in a clear, concise, transparent and easily accessible way. Police Departments have learned the value of having and using good policy. The rest of the city should follow suit.

Like previous comments on goals, policies should be thought of in a cascading fashion. City Council should establish, adopt and publish overarching governing policy. All other policy should fit within the parameters of the governing policy. Next in the cascade is management policy. Following that is operational policy. Most policy in most cities falls into this third cascade.

Cities will survive without improving their policy process, but they will not excel. At the end of my city management career, I adopted the phrase, "Policy First." Before any important decision was considered, the policy implications should be considered and, if needed, policy should be created before the decisions were made. When an item is placed on the City Council agenda, one of the questions that should be answered is whether the action follows policy. If there is no policy, then one should be articulated. Policymaking in most cities today is generally weak.

My assertion is that cities need better policy. They need to have clear policy to guide them and to bring order, predictability and consistency to their work. They need policy around which the City Council can focus their disagreement and debate. City Managers need governing policy to clearly know what the City Council wants and to know what the acceptable parameters of their decision-making authority. To exercise the boldness necessary to excel, City Managers need to be on safe political ground by making it clear that any disagreement with what is being done is an argument with governing policy, not an argument with the person carrying it out. There is much policy work yet to be done.

The best example I can give of good policy work is what we did in Killeen, Texas. For much of my career, I had unsuccessfully searched for a policy model that worked. I found some models that seemed to work in non-profit organizations and a few in school districts, but not in cities. The problem with cities is that they are much more political and much more erratic than those other organizations. Simply put, there are not good city examples to follow. In Killeen, we started with the Financial Policy as it was written into the Comprehensive Annual Financial Report. By expanding work on the Financial Policies, including budgeting targets and process, and bringing them before the City Council in a 3-D process, we were able to get appropriate portions of them adopted as Governing Policy. Having that toehold, we worked on City Council procedures for meetings and protocols for dealing with each other. Then, we expanded it with a section on Executive Directives and Limitations. By the time we were done, we had a manual of Governing Standards and Expectations for which we had a strong Council consensus. Finally, we included a requirement for an annual review so that the policies would stay current and aligned with the changing values of the City Council. Following this work, we brought in a person to assemble all the operating policies scattered throughout the city, update and organize them and place them in the proper cascading order. We linked the policies together and referenced which ones were nested in which. We identified gaps in the cascade and began to fill them in. Then, we located a database program wherein we could insert all the policies so that they could be placed on the city's intranet and be available to all departments and employees. I was proud of this work and believed it to be of great benefit to the city. It began to alter the City Council's focus away from simply disagreeing with each other in uncivil ways to legitimately working through issues to gain consensus.

What are the Characteristics of Good Policy?

Like leadership, expectations exist whether they are formal or informal. Sometimes they exist only unclearly in the mind of some person. Unclear or unknown expectations are poor policy. What are the characteristics of <u>good</u> policy? The traits of good policy include the following:

<u>Clarity.</u> Good policy clarifies purpose. It is clear in language and understanding. It is hard to misinterpret or misunderstand. It adds clarity to direction and action.

<u>Explicitness.</u> It is definite, bold, straightforward, current and relevant. It is reduced to writing. It is official. It is unambiguous.

<u>Brevity.</u> Good policy should be short and direct. Too much language gets confusing.

<u>Empowerment.</u> Policy empowers people to act with creativity and boldness; to feel comfortable in making decisions because they are within the guidelines and inside of the boundaries of explicit policy. Many times, the most empowering policy is one that tells persons what they cannot do rather than what they must do. By articulating what is not acceptable, a great deal of decision-making space is left to exercise creativity and action to accomplish the purpose.

<u>Accountability.</u> Good policy not only empowers people to act; it requires them to do so. It makes them accountable to behave, achieve and accomplish. Good policy creates accountability.

<u>Auditable.</u> Through clarity and accountability, people act on policy. Having done so, their actions can be measured. Good policy will define how and when performance on the policy will be reviewed and evaluated.

<u>Important note of caution:</u> It is possible that some City Managers neglect policy. Maybe it's because they haven't

yet realized its importance to the City Council, or possibly it's because they have realized its importance and they want to avoid being accountable. City Council members should pay close attention to this and correct any problems they encounter.

How Do You Make Good Policy?

To make good policy, a City Council will follow the same basic process as they do for making any other good decision. First, they Discover the facts and gather all the information. Second, they Discuss the issue until all questions have been answered and all points of view have been heard. Third, they Decide. It must be done in that order; it is the 3-D process. To make good decisions and good policy, this process is magic.

How Do You Make Policy Accessible?

To be useful, policy must be accessible. Users of the policy must be able to get to it. Policy documents are living creatures and they are constantly evolving. Consequently, users must have access to the most recent versions of the policy. Departments can be very large and differences between departments are significant. To bring consistency across the municipal enterprise, one must be able to compare policies across department boundaries. This is a very dynamic and challenging process. Paper bound policy books are no longer functionally ideal for this process. Policies are most functional when they are electronically stored, electronically linked and searchable. For internal use, an intranet is ideal. When you're ready to share policies publicly, put them on the internet via your website.

How Can a City Manager Help?

Policymaking is one of the primary responsibilities of the City Council and their role in policymaking is to deal with Governing Policy. Executive Policy supports and operationalizes governing policy and is the responsibility of the City Manager. There are several things a City Manager can do to help the City Council in fulfilling their responsibility to create Governing Policy:

Policy First. City Managers should always be thinking about policy and the policy context of city operations. No matter what issue you're dealing with, you should ask, do we have a governing policy that guides this decision? Even if there is Department Operating Policy that addresses the issue, you must ask if there is an Executive Policy and if there is a Governing Policy in which to nest the Department Operating Policy. If not, don't finish the issue until one has been made. Policy should always come first because it is the primary job of the City Council.

Ideal. In the perfect world, policy should go from top down with Governing, then Executive, then Department/Operating. In the real world and until the policy structure is complete, it won't work that way. There will be cases where Department/ Operating policy exists, but it is not nested. Don't worry about it. When those instances are found, and there will be many of them, create the nesting policy and complete the cascade. Over time, the policy structure will populate and be complete. When that happens, it will become ideal and work from top down.

Create a format and structure. It would be an extraordinary occasion to come into a new city and find a policy structure in place. Don't count on it. You will need to create one and begin to populate it.

Start where you are. If your city has policy that is working well, reformat it into the structure you want to use. If you have an acceptable structure, continue to use it. You will eventually find yourself dealing with contentious issues and you will probably find that there is no governing policy to guide the decision process. This is an ideal time to add to the policy structure.

Respect the Council. Governing Policy belongs to the City Council. The City Manager's job is to make sure the Council sees the value in policy and make sure they have the facts, implications, alternatives and costs associated with their decision. Then, let them make the decision; insist that they make it. Have a system in place to review and confirm or amend it, especially as the personalities on the Council change.

Accountability and focus. Appoint someone to oversee administering policy. This is the only way a City Manager can slug through the policy disorder and detail. A specific person needs to be accountable to get it done.

Reference your policy. As you prepare staff reports, recommendations and proposals, reference back to the supporting policy that guides your recommended action. This will help keep the Council focused on their policy-making role. If any of them disagree with what is being done, the argument should be with the policy, not with you or your actions; it should be with the policy. With a review process in place, the Council will have an opportunity to advocate changing the policy at the right time.

Put review dates on key policies. New people are constantly coming on to the City Council. Current Councilmembers sometimes have a change of heart. There needs to be a time for reviewing policy to make sure it continues to express the will of the City Council. Further, the policy and its process should be included in all orientation briefings for new City Council members. Annual reviews of Governing Policy should be scheduled soon after new Councilmembers are seated.

Advising City Council Regarding their Oversight Responsibility

The City Council's oversight duties require them to give watchful care over the performance of the organization. For the most part, they do this indirectly through the people they appoint to positions of responsibility and trust within the city. Their oversight applies to three general groups: 1) direct reports; 2) appointees to Boards, Commissions and Committees; 3) themselves. The first two groups are obvious, the third group, themselves, not so much. It is true that the voters are the ultimate judge of whether the City Council has done its job, but, in between elections, the Council must judge its own work.

I recall one of my performance evaluations with a City Council. It was among the first with that particular Council and it went well. At the end of the process, one of the Councilmembers said, "Now that we have evaluated you, I'd like you to evaluate us. Can you tell us how we, as a Council, are doing?" The question surprised me. I had been in the profession for a number of years and never had a Council asked me that question. On reflection, I think it was an insightful question that opened the possibility of additional dialog between me and my bosses. However, in the end, only the Council can evaluate its own work and provide governing oversight to the city.

Who Are the City Council's Direct Reports?

The number of direct reports to a City Council is generally quite small. First, there is the City Manager. Second is the City Judge. Pretty much all cities have these two positions. Depending on how the Charter or governing laws are written, there may be other positions that report directly to the City Council. These may include City Auditor, City Attorney, City Clerk or Secretary. If these positions do not report directly to the City Council, then they will fall under the supervision of the City Manager.

Appointees to Boards, Commissions and Committees

The number of people appointed to voluntarily serve in these types of responsibilities can be very large. Typically, the City Manager will appoint a staff liaison to support these individual groups to ensure that they are getting the administrative support they need, that they are complying with required legal parameters and that needed communication between the appointed group and the rest of the city occurs as it should. Occasionally people will think that the staff is responsible for ensuring that the various Boards do their work. This is not the case. Boards are not responsible to the City Manager or his staff; they are responsible to the City Council. The City Council must take on the duty to ensure that their appointees are performing properly.

I recall an instance in one of my cities where the City Council appointed one of its own members to liaison with own appointed boards. It worked reasonably well until one of the boards began to defer its hard decisions to the attending Councilmember, simply because of the presence of a "higher authority." Ultimately, the Council had to remove all Council liaisons from all committees to stop this interference from occurring. So, there may be many ways to accomplish this oversight and the Council will need to find the one that works best for the personalities and circumstances involved.

City Council Overseeing Their Own Work.

As I have previously noted, it is true that the electorate ultimately decides if the City Council is doing a good job. Unfortunately, by the time the electorate makes its decision, it's too late to make meaningful changes to Council process. The interim step, between elections, that should not be overlooked, is for the Council to evaluate its own work. By so doing, they will critique and improve their own internal processes and governing methods.

How Does the City Council Perform Oversight?

The question has been asked, "If you don't know where you're going, how will you know when you've arrived?" This is the key to performing oversight and performance evaluation of any kind. It must begin with clarity on the front end of what the expectations are before the work is begun. Absent this, it will likely degenerate into an evaluation of personalities rather than performance.

> Overseeing Direct Reports. At the beginning of a rating period, the City Council should set clear and realistic expectations. Ideally, the person being evaluated should have a say in those expectations and should agree to them. The end of the process should be quite simple by answering these questions: Did the person meet the predetermined expectations or not? Did they achieve the goals or not? By setting clear expectations up front, the Council has already set the form and format of the evaluation at the end of the process. The City Council should not overlook all their direct reports by placing all their attention on the City Manager. This occurs more often than it should. All the direct reports deserve the Council's attention.
>
> Overseeing Boards, Commissions and Committees. The duties, expectations and behavior requirements for the members of Boards, Commissions and Committees should be set forth in the ordinances or resolutions that created them. The City Council should require periodic, at least annual, reports from their Chairpersons of Boards, Commissions and Committees to ensure that the individual members are performing according to their expectations and statutory duty. Attendance, participation and ethical compliance reports should be received by the City Council before considering the reappointment of any person. In some cases, it would be wise to ask the

committee for a plan of work for the upcoming year. That enables the Council to evaluate accomplishments at the end of the year based on what the committee said they would do. Many times, the Council will place increased emphasis on the Planning and Zoning Commission because of their heavy and sometimes controversial workload, to the detriment of other groups. So, a comment, like the one about direct reports, is justified here: The Council should give due attention to all of its Board, Commission and Committee appointments.

Overseeing their own work. Just like the others, a City Council should be clear about what it wants to accomplish and how the process of functioning as a team will work. This is required before it can evaluate its own work. In my experience, this is best done by 1) establishing a policy of Governing Standards and Expectations to clarify decorum and functional process and, 2) setting goals for itself to achieve during the rating period. Having the goals, standards and expectations in place will make it possible to periodically evaluate progress.

Invariably, a renegade Councilperson will not cooperate with this type of process, believing that she is accountable only to the voters and not to her colleagues on the City Council. In that case, the Council has limited options that include 1) simply being transparent about the process and outcomes so that the voters have something on which to base their decisions, 2) public censure, in difficult cases, 3) removal from office, in extreme cases and in accordance with applicable Charter or legal provisions.

I have worked with several Councils who have tried to evaluate their own work, but I have never seen one be totally successful. It has usually broken down over a conflict of political philosophies masked as personality conflict. When that happens, the process becomes painful, and it is usually dropped. Just because it's difficult doesn't mean Council shouldn't be doing it.

Overseeing Governing Policy. There are several ways the City Council can ensure that its governing policies are being followed:

First, staff reports are typically prepared for all items on the City Council agenda. A section should be included in each staff report that identifies the applicable governing policy and certifies compliance.

Second, governing policy should receive an annual review by the City Council, at which time compliance and problems can be discussed.

Third, the City Auditor or other third-party reviewer can be assigned to conduct detailed reviews of specific policies and then report back to the City Council.

How Can a City Manager Help?

Oversight is one of the primary responsibilities of the City Council. The Council's role is to focus its oversight attention on their direct reports, their Boards and Commissions and on themselves. There are several things that a City Manager can do to help the City Council in fulfilling its Oversight responsibility:

Have no fear. Don't be afraid of, or avoid, the City Council evaluating your work.

Do the front-end work. Help the City Council to do their duty on the front end by asking them questions about how they will judge your performance and what they expect from you. Assist them to get their answers into clear, concise written format. If they are not good at doing this, prepare the kind of clarifying performance expectations you would like to see from them; present it to them and let them revise and confirm it.

<u>Don't leave anyone out.</u> Help them to treat all their direct reports in a similar manner.

<u>Be easy to work with.</u> Be open and accept their evaluation and their criticism in a constructive way. Respond to it by amending your behavior.

<u>Clarify ordinances for Boards.</u> Ensure that the ordinances and resolutions that create Boards, Commissions and Committees are explicit enough to create performance expectations that can be evaluated by the City Council. If improvement is in order, take the initiative to make the changes.

<u>Assist with reports.</u> Instruct your staff to create valuable reports from the Boards, Commissions and Committees that will assist the City Council to evaluate the effectiveness of their performance.

<u>Establish governing policy.</u> Assist the City Council in establishing Governing Policies and Standards so that they can objectively evaluate their own behavior and performance.

<u>Establish annual goals.</u> Assist the City Council in establishing annual goals for themselves. These will likely dovetail with the work expected by the Council of the City Manager but should also include a "Policy Calendar" that specifies the policy issues the Council intends to address throughout the year.

<u>Coach.</u> Communicate with the City Council regarding these principles relating to their fourth duty and make sure they agree with them. Don't forget your staff either. Your Assistant City Managers, and others, need to understand these principles as well; mentor them.

<u>Train.</u> Conduct or provide training, especially for newly elected City Council members, that make these duties and practices clear to them.

Advising the City Council Regarding Their Required Ministerial Tasks

A ministerial task for the City Council is one that is required of them by law or by custom to perform, and which is routine in nature and of relatively low importance compared to the other duties of the City Council. It often has little to do with governance and more to do with management. Examples might include things like canvassing the results of an election, approving lists of bills for payment, giving approval to apply for a grant, approving already pre-approved budgeted purchases, receiving and reviewing investment reports or approving the issuance of requests for bid proposals. There are scores of possible examples. In fact, my experience from working in seven jurisdictions is that ministerial tasks consume a majority portion of a City Council's agenda.

The danger is that, not knowing any better, the City Council may think low importance ministerial tasks are the most important things they must do. The big question is, if the City Council spends most of its precious time on ministerial tasks, when will they have time to do the important work? When will they work their way through necessary governing policy? When will they define their city's future, their vision? When will they create strategy for achieving their vision? If they don't do the important things, who will? Ministerial tasks masquerade themselves as oversight duties, and they are not. Even though ministerial tasks must be done, they are, in fact, very big wasters of City Council time. The other four City Council duties are more important than ministerial tasks.

If you were to use a time management matrix[3] with four quadrants (Urgent and Important, Not Urgent but Important, Urgent but not Important, and Not Urgent or Important), the ministerial tasks required by law would be in the quadrant labeled urgent but not important.

---

[3] For informative reading regarding the time management matrix, sometimes referred to as the Eisenhower Method, I recommend the 7 Habits of Highly Effective People by Dr Stephen R Covey.

Ministerial tasks required by custom, but not the law, would be in the quadrant labeled not urgent and not important. The issue for the City Council becomes one of prioritizing their work and managing their time so that important issues get addressed.

I recall an experience from my first city. Looking back on it, the City Council spent most of its time on ministerial items, including reviewing and re-doing the work of the Planning Commission. Because we were a very fast-growing city, every Council agenda had several Planning and Zoning actions to consider. After more than five years of this time-consuming work, one of my Department Heads calculated the average dismissal time of the weekly City Council meeting to be after 12:30 am. Occasionally, a meeting would go to 2:00 am. Those meetings were on Tuesday evening, starting at 5:00 pm, after the regular workday was over. Work done after about 10:00 pm was inefficient anyway because no one was thinking straight. On Wednesday morning, we would hold staff meeting to set the agenda and prepare for the next City Council meeting. (Agenda publication requirements gave us two days, at best, to perform follow-up research and prepare responses for unanswered questions from the previous meeting as well as to prepare new agenda items for the next meeting.) We were all burning out, becoming modern, real-life zombies. The City Council was using small town methods of doing business even though they had grown into a medium sized city. The unimportant work was getting done but there was no time left for the important. I was too young in the profession to tell the City Council they needed to change the way they were doing their business. On top of that misapplication of Council time, they decided to form committees aligned after the various operational missions of the city. They wanted to oversee city operations but, in hindsight, it was the wrong way to do it. The committees started out with the goal of keeping Council informed of operational detail, but became super-managers, requiring the staff to get their operational marching orders from the committee rather than the appropriate chain of command. Those dysfunctional committees gave me a career-long aversion to Council committees and helped me form more clear ideas about the duties of the elected and appointed officers of the city. It also helped me find better ways to get the public's work done. So... when did the City Council have time for the committee work? Because they all had regular jobs in addition to their City Council duties, the committee meetings were scheduled before and after normal working hours, adding to everyone's burn-out. Thank goodness no one had the physical energy to carry that committee schedule for very long. Talk about misplaced priorities; talk about an extraordinary exercise in ministerial trivia. This whole process was a dysfunctional shipwreck. I wish I had known then what I know now and could go back and fix it.

Conservatively estimating time expended, I have spent more than two years of my life in formal City Council meetings. The only reason it's not more than two years is because my meetings in Polk County, Iowa, were short; they were minutes, not hours. I don't even want to begin to think about the additional years spent in preparing for those meetings. There were times when I thought I would live forever because many of those meetings seemed to last an eternity. The ones that seemed to last the longest were the ones where we spent too much time on trivial, unnecessary, repetitive ministerial nonsense. The meetings where we did real work and made good progress on important topics were enjoyable for me.

So, how do you overcome the abusing pitfalls of ministerial tasks? The answer: delegate and manage by exception.

With the right discussion and work effort, the City Council can identify the criteria by which they would normally approve a ministerial item. The criteria can be placed in a policy. The staff can screen the ministerial items to ensure they fall within policy. If they do, they can be certified by the staff and placed on a consent agenda for the Council to be approved all together in one motion. This process uses as little City Council time as possible and still gets the job done within parameters set by Council. If an item does not fall within policy parameters, it will be placed on a regular agenda where the Council can take all the time necessary to resolve it. The City Auditor (or other designee, if there is no Auditor) can periodically audit these types of actions and independently certify to the City Council that their policy is being followed. This process can be used on all ministerial items.

Let's talk about Consent Agendas. A Consent Agenda is a single item placed on the City Council agenda which has multiple topics. With one motion and vote, all the topics on that item are approved, without discussion. The topics of the Consent Agenda are non-controversial, comply with preset policy criteria, and have the unanimous agreement of the City Council as determined in a work session or first reading of the item.

Consent Agendas make a lot of sense. So, why are they not more broadly used and why do some City Council members object to their use? Typically, I think it is because 1) they do not understand the principle of placing their limited time on the most important things first; or, 2) they do not know what the most important things are; they make the mistake of thinking all things are of equal importance; or 3) their constituents do not understand these things and give them a hard time, intimidating them into poor governing practices. Many times, I have heard constituents publicly criticize City Council members for being "rubber stamps" or for not asking enough questions, etc. Rather than exercise the leadership necessary to inform their constituents, some Council members find it easier to conform to the public image required of them.

Here are some additional practices that make Consent Agendas more palatable. Two of the Charters in cities I managed required City Council agenda items to receive two readings before they were voted on. An item was supposed to be on the agenda for two separate meetings, giving the Council time to think about it and giving the public time to know about it. In both of those cities, the practice had developed to waive the requirement for two readings by declaring the items as "emergencies" and passing them on one reading. In one of those cities, I advised the City Council to change their practice and honor the Charter by having two separate readings. This helped make the Council meetings much smoother and relationships more congenial. We organized the agenda with a three action sections. The first of these was for the Consent Agenda, where all items that had been previously reviewed and agreed upon could be passed without further discussion and on one motion. The second section was for Second Readings. These were items that had been previously presented and discussed but not agreed upon. These items would be given further deliberation and then voted on. The third section was for First Readings, where new items for a future meeting would be introduced and discussed if the Council had questions. If the Council was satisfied with the issue, one of them would make a motion to include it on either the Consent Agenda or Second Reading for their next meeting. Initially, one might think that this process would take up even more time, but it didn't because it satisfied the Council's need to be perceived as being informed, engaged and in control. And they were. It also helped the most interested of constituents to better understand both the Council process and the details of the issues. In the cities where the Charter did not require two readings and I found the Council objecting to creating a policy requiring two readings, alternating work sessions in between regular meetings accomplished the same thing. By helping the City Council manage their time in this manner, we made time available for them to work on the more important items.

How Can a City Manager Help?

Approving ministerial items is a basic duty of a City Council. However, uncontrolled ministerial tasks can be a major waste of City Council time. There are several things a City Manager can do to help the City Council fulfill their duty regarding ministerial tasks and help them to waste as little time as possible in the process. Those things include:

Identify ministerial items. Go back over some old agendas and identify the recurring ministerial items that the City Council has considered.

Create policy. Ensure that the Council has adopted a policy for dealing with individual ministerial tasks. They need to articulate the parameters within which they would normally approve the item. Ensure that the policy is followed so that the Council has confidence in it.

Use a Consent Agenda. Overcome any objections that may exist and assist the City Council to effectively use a Consent Agenda.

Do first things first. Make sure you know what the most important things are. Do them first. Don't let the urgent and the trivial overtake the important. If you don't help the City Council to manage their time and do their job, who will?

It Is Simple, Not Easy

All of this sounds simple enough; I assure you that it is much harder in practice. Even though governing is on a higher order than managing, my observation is that some City Council members, and there are always some, cannot grasp the bigger picture of their governing role. Instead of committing time and energy to their strategic, high-level responsibilities, which no one else can do for them, they want to focus attention on operational detail. Taken too far, it turns into the kind of interference prohibited by most City Charters. Countless times I have heard this, or something akin to it: "I understand that my role is policy and yours is management, but…"; or "I am not trying to micromanage, but…." Anything a City Council member says after the word "but" is out of order. There is a clear process for city Councilmembers to get what they want; they must have the cooperation of their colleagues and they must follow approved policy and process. It is not as easy as you may think it should be and it always takes longer than you think it should. The challenge of this Charter-defined way of doing City business becomes magnified when Councilmembers cannot demonstrate the kind of leadership that fosters cooperation with their colleagues.

Often, the electorate does not help this process. They will call their elected Councilmember to complain about potholes and barking dogs rather than calling the city agency charged with fixing those problems. Many times I have heard citizens tell Councilmembers that they did not elect the dog catcher, they elected the Councilmember, and they expect the elected official to solve the problem. Because the elected official is hesitant to tell the constituent that barking dogs and potholes are not his job, it encourages the Councilmember to get involved in the operating detail. If they try to give the dog catcher an order to pick up a barking dog, they are subject to losing their office for violation of the Charter. It takes a while for elected officials to learn to inform and lead their constituency. Some never do. Those that never do drive their City Manager nuts. City Managers need to set up responsive systems inside of their operations to handle routine calls for service so that City Councilmembers have confidence in referring their constituency to use them, or they can pass the service complaints along to those systems themselves. There is much work to be done by elected officials and City Managers to teach the constituency how city government works.

Governing happens in the big picture. It is directional; it is not precise. It is general, not specific. Management implements the big picture in precise ways; there are always many ways to implement the big picture. City Councils must govern. City Managers must manage. Otherwise, the city will flounder. Approving Goals and Change Targets is part of Governing. Generally, governing is not natural for City Councilmembers so the City Manager must coach, teach and advise them.

In Summary, How to Advise the City Council

This chapter has covered the second duty of a City Manager, Advising the City Council. Good City Managers, like all good employees, do not wait to be told what to do. They anticipate the needs of their employer and are proactive in their service. The duty of a City Manager to advise the City Council involves informing, warning, cautioning, coaching and, at the right time, recommending.

Before a City Manager can be an effective advisor to the City Council, he must understand clearly what the duties of the City Council entails and how that differs from his own duties. Much of the conflict that arises between Councils and Managers is generated by one or both parties not understanding what their respective duties are. The duties of a City Council include leadership, approving high level goals, setting governing policy, providing oversight, and performing required ministerial acts. The better a City Manager understands these elected duties, the better she can fulfill her own duty to advise the City Council.

Further, to be an effective advisor, it is important for a City Manager to understand how and why it is difficult for members of the community to serve on the City Council. Those reasons include the complexity of required decisions, the unexpectedly high costs of doing public business, the non-partisan but political nature of the work, the unrealistic expectations of both the Council members and the citizens they represent, and sometimes the lack of effective professional staff support.

One of the most important tools to be used in advising the City Council is the 3-D process. This group process includes 1) Discovery – learning every necessary thing about a decision that needs to be made, 2) Debate – making sure all questions are answered and every opinion heard; and 3) Decide – bringing the issue to a conclusion by voting. It is vital that the steps be done in order. Otherwise, it is like fire, ready, aim instead of ready, aim, fire.

In the chapter, more detailed suggestions have been made for advising on each of the five City Council duties.

It's time to move on to the third duty of a City Manager.

MANAGING

City Operations

Managing City Operations

The City Manager's Third Duty

If you were to ask almost any City Manager in the country what they did, the answer would invariably be this: manage the operations of the city. Some might give you a variant of the same answer, such as carry out the policies and directives of the City Council. At the end of the day, their answer would mean making sure that the work of the city gets done.

In one of the many State City Management Association training sessions I attended, a speaker taught us that the word "manage" comes from the Italian "Maneggiare," to handle or train horses, and from the Latin, "Manus," or hand. The idea is that of a handler, someone who controls for an outcome. So, City Managers handle the business of the city. They control for a desired outcome. They get the job done.

Now, the exact job you do, how well you exercise leadership, how well you advise the City Council, how well you treat people in the process, and how well people may like you are all significant. But no single thing is more important than simply getting the city's work done. If this duty is not performed well, excellent performance on the other duties won't matter much.

So, in the next several sections, I will dissect the process by which cities are managed. From my experience and perspective, I will explain how managing city operations can best be accomplished and how to get this important work done.

What Cities do

Putting first things first, I must be very clear on what the work of cities is. Even though not all cities provide all the services described here, all cities do most of what is described here. There are, therefore, many professions and specialties to support those services. Cities have lawyers, engineers, planners, accountants and technology specialists. They have plumbers, electricians, carpenters, concrete finishers and laborers. They have truck drivers and heavy equipment operators. They have call-takers, nurses and sometimes doctors. Cities have administrative specialists, supervisors and managers at all levels. They have communication specialists, videographers and photographers. They have emergency medical technicians and paramedics. They have evidence technicians, detectives, law enforcement officers, jailers and firefighters. They have code enforcement officers, chemists, printers, professional golfers, swimmers, athletes and recreation specialists of all kinds. They have mechanics, auto body technicians, janitors, HVAC technicians and laborers. They have agronomists, arborists and master gardeners. And many more.

City Managers need to have an appreciation for all these skills and functions. They need to know a little bit about a lot of things to ask the right questions and provide leadership, guidance and good decision-making for the organization.

For all the aforementioned city professions, many departments and divisions exist into which their work is divided and managed. There are many ways of structuring and organizing this work. I have found that the best way is to break the work of cities into five basic categories of services because, by organizing in this fashion, related functions can be grouped together to create synergy and subordinate leadership can be selected to manage portions of the bigger mission. Those five categories are:

1. Public Works
2. Public Safety
3. Recreation
4. Community and Economic Development and
5. Support Services

For further clarity, it is important to understand that for each of the five categories, one should think of their work in two parts: operations and capital. Operations is the day-to-day functioning. It includes people costs, materials, supplies, and capital outlay (purchases of relatively small and inexpensive equipment, not to be confused with Capital Projects). It is the daily programing of services. From a budgeting perspective, it is the annually repeating cost of providing the service. The second part is the Capital (meaning Capital Projects) side of providing the service. The term "Capital Projects" relates to the hard infrastructure necessary to provide the public service. "Infrastructure" is things such as real estate, buildings and structures of all kinds, pipelines, roads and bridges and major pieces of equipment. From a budgeting standpoint, capital items are high dollar, one-time expenditures which sometimes span more than one fiscal year. Generally, the dividing line between capital outlay (an operating expense) and capital projects (a capital expense) is $100,000, although the amount may vary depending on the city and its individual policy. Operations are paid for out of the annual repeating, current revenue stream of a city. Capital is paid for primarily from borrowing, where the principal and interest on the loan are paid for from the current revenue stream of a city. When managing a city, it is important to keep these two parts, capital and operating, separate from each other in your thought process, in the budget and in the actual organization structure. Year by year, operating costs can be compared, and variations can be examined for growth, efficiency and consistency. Continuous improvement requires the ability to dissect performance versus cost, make comparisons, and experiment with changes and new methods of doing the work. If Capital Projects are co-mingled with Operations, you lose the ability to make those important comparisons. You also cloud public transparency.

Now, I will review each of these five basic categories in more detail by placing the next level of service functions within the five categories. I freely admit that unique requirements and specific management preferences may encourage the placement of some functions in different categories than those I suggest here. All other things being equal, this is how I would structure the organization of a city:

1. Public Works
Services provided under this broad category include:

Water. Water services may be divided into three general categories, including:

Culinary water. This includes the development of water rights and raw water sources, the transportation of raw water, the treatment and purification of treated water and all the support and business processes that make it work.
Wastewater. This includes the collection of used and polluted water (commonly referred to as wastewater) through a system of pipes and pump stations, pre-treatment of industrial discharge, treatment of wastewater back to pure standards, disposal of sludge and solids and possibly reuse of treated water.
Storm Water. Storm water is water that falls from the sky on to, primarily, impervious areas such as roofs, driveways, streets and parking lots. It runs off those impervious surfaces at greater rates than it would from a natural, pervious surface, and that turns it into flood water. To prevent it from creating property damage and danger to people, this water is collected through surface and piped drains. The water is detained or retained, sometimes treated, then discharged into a natural water course at rates not greater than the natural runoff would have been. Storm water assets, such as detention

basins, may sometimes have dual use as recreation facilities.

Streets. Everyone is familiar with streets and most people use them every day without thinking twice. Streets may be paved or unpaved. They may be paved with bituminous or concrete pavement. The street system is more than pavement. It also includes signs, signals (including all the electronics that make signals work and coordinate with each other) and markings; concrete curbs, gutters, drainage-ways and sometimes sidewalks; alleys, bridges, overpasses and similar structures. Sometimes a street system will also include designated bicycle paths and routes.

Solid Waste. It has always been amazing to me to see how much paper, cardboard, plastic, glass, metal, construction debris, yard waste, bulky waste, appliance and bio waste we produce. Solid Waste is the service of collecting, transferring, transporting, landfilling, composting and recycling this material. It is one of the most vital and under-appreciated services that cities provide.

2. Public Safety

Services provided under this broad category include the following:

Police. These services are intended to enforce laws and provide even-handed safety to all residents. Most people understand enforcement of traffic laws; police services also include enforcement of criminal violations of local and state law. To support this effort, police departments provide traffic, patrol, and criminal investigations. They conduct covert operations, high risk arrests and special operations. They provide evidence collection, analysis, storage and management. They operate holding facilities for arrestees and, sometimes, full-service jails. Forensics and records management are essential support functions. They have extensive training programs to ensure top performance and mitigate an ever-increasing legal liability. Many police officers spend a significant portion of their time writing reports and testifying in court. To function effectively, police departments are required to communicate effectively, have extensive public information programs and develop effective neighborhood relations programs. Managing police operations is made more complex by the 24/7 nature of the work.

Fire. With Fire Departments, citizens are primarily paying for a state of readiness to respond to emergencies such as fires, auto crashes, high angle rescue, confined space emergencies and medical (described separately) emergencies. They are also responsible for arson investigations and enforcing the fire code. Like police departments, fire departments have very extensive training requirements. In very small jurisdictions, fire services are often "volunteer," meaning part-time or part-paid. Larger cities have full-time fire and rescue operations. In the latter cases, firefighters typically work a 24-hour shift which is generally thought of in three sections. The first 8-hour section is active service where they are training and ensuring equipment is functional and ready. The second section is down time where they prepare meals, watch TV and generally relax from the training and active section of the day. The third section is sleeping in the dormitory part of the fire station. During all three of these daily sections, they are subject to responding to calls should they occur. Following the 24 hours on duty, they have 48 hours off duty. Because of 24 on - 48 off scheduling and considering paid time off, it typically takes four people to staff every required position in a fire station. Because of OSHA requirements and NFPA recommended standards, there is constant pressure on City Managers for increased staffing in fire departments.

Emergency Medical Service. Most, but not all, fire departments have combined emergency medical services with fire and rescue services. This is called "fire-based medical" service. In departments under this configuration, about 80% of the total Fire Department emergency calls will be medically related. Responders can be certified at either an Emergency Medical Technician (EMT) level or a Paramedic level. The primary difference is that Paramedics can provide advanced life support; they can administer drugs and better respond to cardiac arrest than EMTs. It is not uncommon to see both an ambulance and a fire truck responding to medical emergencies. This is because most emergency medical calls require more than two people to handle them and oftentimes fire trucks can get to the scene before an ambulance. Trained personnel are typically staffing all the apparatus and are interchangeable in their assignments. Interchanging is not always easy because of work rules and labor contracts, but it is possible.

For departments that do not have fire-based medical, it is typical to see a contract with a private ambulance company to both respond to emergencies and provide transport to hospitals. A great deal of flexibility can be used in determining levels of service, response times, etc., when using this form of service. Keep in mind, even when EMS services are contracted out, fire personnel may, and typically do, still respond to medical emergencies to provide fast response or to assist the contractor with difficult cases.

Protective Inspections. Cities have responsibility to inspect a great number of things. The inspections I'm referring to in this section are related to building safety and those that protect the public from possible harm, not those that simply enhance the quality of life. Services that are included in the protective category include health, electrical, plumbing, fire, structural (load, wind, earthquake) and, in general, all building codes. These types of codes are created nationally or internationally created and adopted locally. They are constantly being updated and are intended to prevent a life-threatening event from occurring rather than responding to it after it has occurred. Municipalities provide inspections to ensure compliance with the codes that hedge against risk and protect the public from a possible future harm. Often, these services are found in the Community and Economic Development category; I personally believe they belong in the Public Safety category.

3. Recreation

Unlike the previous two basic categories of service (Public Works and Public Safety) which are more "essential," this one is more discretionary. That does not mean that it is unnecessary or unimportant. On the contrary, Recreation Services are vital to the quality of life, the physical and emotional well-being of the people in a community. In the hierarchy of needs, they often come below the physical requirements of having water, health and safety. Services included in this basic category are:

Parks and Open Space. Parks are developed for a variety of uses. Some of them provide a venue for sports activities such as baseball or soccer. Some provide for general exercise by having trails, skating facilities or exercise facilities. Some have fishing ponds. There are many other special purpose parks as well. Maintenance is always required in a developed park for both physical facilities, playgrounds, grass and trees. If a park does not have a developed purpose, it may be a greenbelt or general open space. This type of space generally requires less maintenance attention, but always requires some.

Recreation. Providing recreation services almost always accompanies the use of parks space. Sometimes it requires a separate building or recreation center. Cities can choose to directly provide the recreation service, or they may contract or delegate it to non-profit organizations that specialize in, mostly, youth sports activities. Various levels of management are required for the management of recreation programs.

Aquatics. This includes swimming pools, water parks and splash pads. Depending on the location, it may also include canoeing and other water sports. For many cities, these are seasonal activities.

Senior Centers. Most cities provide meeting and activity spaces and programing for senior citizens. This is often accompanied by a coordinated effort with federal grant programs for meals and transportation.

Community Centers. These are general meeting spaces for people of all ages and the Centers are generally configured in a very flexible manner to support some sports activities as well as meeting spaces for clubs and groups. Seniors could meet in these Centers. Youth and after-school programs could also be conducted in them.

Recreation Centers. These buildings are specifically constructed, and specific programing provided, to support sports activities such as basketball, handball, volleyball, yoga, floor exercises, strength training and cardiovascular exercise and a variety of other activities.

Golf Courses. Public golf courses provide this specific type of recreation to a portion of the city's population. Most city golf courses are set up in enterprise funds to be self-supporting after the borrowing required for the capital expense of building the course is paid off. Golf courses, while owned by a city, may be operated and managed by either the city or by a private management company under contract to the city.

Libraries. With the constant advances in electronic media, the way we get our information is changing. Libraries still play an important role in the quality of life in a community. Leading edge libraries are making sure that their services include not only printed material, but also electronic materials and electronic access. One of the biggest current challenges to libraries is the indigent homeless populations in Cities who use the libraries as day shelters and make it more difficult for other citizens to use the facilities for their original purposes.

Animal Zoos and Parks. A few, mostly larger, cities own and operate zoos. An increasing number of cities are providing parks where owners can allow their dogs to run and exercise unrestrained. These are commonly referred to as dog parks. Management of Animal Services and Animal Control could fall under several of the basic categories of service (Public Safety or Community Development), and they could be nested, as I have suggested here, in Recreation as well.

Events. Most communities have events and celebrations that enhance the quality of life within that community and celebrate their history. These events also provide a unique character to the city and help make it stand out from other communities. Typical events include Independence Day celebrations, Founders Day activities and holiday parades, etc. Unique events can include things like rodeos, Mardi Gras, New Year's Eve at Time Square and Dyeing the Chicago River green for St Patrick's Day, etc.

4. Community and Economic Development

Looking ahead, encouraging the development of a tax base that supports future vision, and providing amenities that assist to empower the less affluent parts of the community are the hallmarks of this category.

Planning and Zoning. Most cities have a system of land use designed to protect the value and rights of all property and property owners. This is called zoning. Zoning allows specific uses in specific areas so that abutting uses are compatible. There is an entire system of geographic designations as well as rules to go along with the different designations. There are well-defined procedures, public disclosures and public participation required by the processes. This zoning process is supported by a massive planning effort for both long-term and current time-frames. Economic Development. Cities receive major portions of their revenue from property tax and sales tax. A very few cities also receive a local income tax. Building these tax bases is the mission of Economic Development. Although cities cannot create or control the local economy, they can do certain things to influence it. For example, they can actively recruit new business to locate within their jurisdiction. They can encourage those businesses with a limited number of incentives. Today, it has become common for cities to compete for the location of new business into their jurisdiction or to retain existing business and discourage them from relocating. These services may be provided either directly by the city or by contract with another entity, typically a public Economic Development Corporation. This topic will be covered in more detail later.

Business Support. Most cities support business (and, therefore, their own tax base) through memberships or contributions to the local Chamber of Commerce, through purchasing preferences for local businesses, etc.

Conference Centers. Most states authorize local governments to assess a bed tax on local hotels. That bed tax, sometimes called a Hotel Occupancy Tax or HOT, is used to encourage tourism and use of the hotels and restaurants in that area. Conference Centers are a common way to attract visitors as are museums, historical sites, and local events. These types of things are often supported, in whole or in part, from bed taxes.

Community Development Grants. There was a time when the federal government provided numerous grants to local governments. The vestige of that era is the Community Development Block Grant. This grant is received from the Federal Government and used for various projects in low- or moderate-income neighborhoods. It has numerous limitations and reporting requirements. If a city is large enough, it will be a direct recipient of this funding. If not, it will receive a proportional allocation from another responsible unit of government. For direct recipients, the program is administered by the city and included in the city's annual audit for accountability purposes back to the federal government.

Public Transportation. Transit systems of various sorts are used by cities. These may vary from Dial-a-ride systems to fixed route bus systems, to subways and light rail. Sometimes, cities will have combinations of all the above. Although these systems are often thought of as supporting the low-income population, they can also be used by the affluent for conservation and as a practical, timesaving means of getting around. For the most part, these systems are heavily subsidized by the federal government but there is always a local share required, along with the responsibility of administrating the program.

Public Housing. Many cities have Housing Authorities which provide rental housing to low- and moderate-income people, with some specialized in providing housing to disabled and senior populations. The Housing Authority may be part of the city organization. More often, it is a separate entity that is only related to the city because it shares the name of the city as part of its own title. For the most part, Housing Authorities constructed their facilities from grants received from the federal government while operating expenses are covered from the rents received. The rents are often not at market rates but are adjusted, according to federal rules, by the renter's ability to pay.

Emergency Shelter Grants (ESG) which are funded by the federal government and administered by the city for the purpose of assisting the homeless population and Section 8 vouchers. Again, these are provided by the federal government and administered under detailed guidelines by the city for the use of low- and moderate-income persons.

Sister Cities. As a good will gesture and as part of their economic development efforts, many cities have adopted sister cities. This is where a city reaches out to a city in another country to develop a special relationship with them. Visits are made by one city to the other through official channels and through youth programs. Sometimes the costs associated with these relationships are part of the official city budget and sometimes they are financially supported by the participants. Sometimes the administration of the program is borne by the city and sometimes it is borne by volunteers.

Volunteers. Every city has some form of volunteerism. In some cases, it is very extensive and requires an office of fulltime employees to support it. In other cases, it is small and occurs almost spontaneously. In most cases, the city will contribute part of the budget to support whatever the volunteers are tasked with accomplishing whether that task is a city event or helping to achieve part of the primary mission of the city such as being a Ranger at the golf course, an usher at a city venue or serving on a Board or Commission. Volunteers provide important service to the city; they must be managed and there are liabilities and costs associated with volunteer programs.

5. Support Services

The final basic category of city service is Support Services. Unlike the previous four categories, this one does not have an independent life. The entire reason for this category to exist is to serve the other four. If the other four did not exist, there would be no reason for this one to exist. All the functions in the other four categories have common requirements. They all need financial management. They all need human resource support. They all need information technology. The most efficient way to provide these services to those line departments is to do it centrally. Indeed, when a city begins to break down and fail in its function, each department will begin to build up, and duplicate, support services within itself. This is because it must have the service and cannot function properly without it. When there are financial stresses, it is common to see the support services reduced in both budget and personnel to prevent cutting the line functions. This is a very short-term solution and cannot be maintained in the long run. It is far better to view the support functions as an integral part of the line service. If using a functional cost accounting system in the city, the costs of the support services can, and should, be assigned to each line department. Here are the services of this category:

Finance. This is the support service that provides the city and all its departments with financial services such as accounting, purchasing, accounts receivable, accounts payable, cash handling and investing, budgeting, bonding, payroll and financial reporting. These services are essential to good management and decision-making.

Human Resources. Recruiting new employees, testing, selection, training, all aspects of discipline, benefits management and employee records management are all key components of this service.

Risk Management. Liability and property insurance, automobile safety, minimizing personal injury and property loss through training and awareness are all part of this important function.

Information Technology. The world hardly moves without being connected or served in some way through technology. Cities are no different. When the computers go down, the work stops. Processes managed by hand rather than technology are very costly. There is general technology that supports all city functions and there are department specific technologies that aid in their work. All departments need to be connected to the people they serve; the city needs to be connected to its constituency and to the world. This service includes not only computers and programs, but also telecommunications and Geographic Information Systems (GIS). Technology changes rapidly. It is hard to keep up with and stay current, and technology is one of the most important tools that municipalities have.

I recall an interchange I had with a Council member when the internet was just becoming functional and available to cities. This Council member was critical of my desire to establish a web page and internet presence. He said that such "toys" were expensive and unnecessary to the proper functioning of the city. I told him that they were not toys, but tools. Time has proven that he could not have been more wrong. Today, cities, like most enterprises, could not even survive without their technology.

Fleet Maintenance. Cities own significant equipment. Cars, pickup trucks, dump trucks, fire trucks, ambulances, backhoes, graders, dozers, construction equipment of all kinds, vacuum trucks, elevated platform trucks, buses and much more are part of the typical city's fleet. Sometimes, airplanes and helicopters are part of the fleet. If you can imagine a piece of equipment, cities probably own or use it. If it has wheels or tracks, it is referred to as rolling stock. If it has a motor or gas engine or is an unpowered piece of equipment such as a trailer, it is simply equipment. Purchasing, inventorying, maintaining, fueling and disposing of the fleet are critical services to the primary functions of the city.

Building Maintenance. Like any substantial business, Cities own buildings to support their operations. These include City Halls for office work mostly, courthouses, jails, police stations, fire stations, maintenance garages, storage facilities, warehouses, water treatment plants, wastewater treatment plants and solid waste transfer stations, etc. Most of these buildings need janitorial-type service, heating and air conditioning service, and parking lot repair. All of them need roof repair. Keeping these assets in good condition is important to the workforce and the public, and it saves taxpayer money in the long run. It is always easier and cheaper to fix a small problem before it becomes a big problem. Yet deferred building maintenance is a real problem in most cities.

Communication. In today's world, people want to know what's going on. Citizens and taxpayers want to know what their city is doing and how they are spending their money. With the Open Records and Open Meetings laws that have been passed in most states, cities are obligated to provide a great deal of information. They should do it anyway, required or not. Relating to and providing information to the press -- newspaper, TV, and radio -- is an important part of this function. In the old days, mass media was the primary way for cities to communicate with their residents. That is no longer true. Like other businesses and institutions, through technology cities can communicate directly with their constituency. Most medium-sized or larger cities can broadcast public meetings over cable channels on the TV or to live stream over the internet. Some have studios where they produce informative content about the city, its services and issues, to broadcast or stream to their people.

Citizen engagement, where city officials go out to directly listen to and talk with residents about important issues is part of Communications. Supporting speaker's bureaus and neighborhood meetings is important to citizen engagement as well.

Internal communication with its own workforce is another key component of city Communications.

Engineering. Occasionally, an engineer specialty such as structural engineering or electronic engineering is required but the bulk of city work requires civil engineering. Civil Engineering service supports all public works and, generally, the management of new capital improvements. Many times, engineering is located inside of the public works department. I have it listed in Support Services because it is not a primary mission of the city; it supports the primary Public Works mission.

Legal. We live in a litigious society and just about everything cities do has legal boundaries and implications. These conditions require that a city employ legal services. In smaller cities, legal service may be provided by contract with private attorneys. In larger cities, the largest "law firm" in town may be inside of city hall. Typically, attorneys are assigned to departments depending on their needs. Sometimes an attorney will be assigned to more than one department. When it comes to specialty issues such as defending against a lawsuit covered by an insurance company, or special environmental or civil rights litigation, outside counsel may be retained even when the city has its own lawyers. Every contract and every item going before the City Council will get a legal review before it is acted on. Under various city charters, the City Attorney may work directly for the City Council and be an organizational equal to the City Manager, or the City Attorney may work directly for the City Manager and serve the City Council through the Manager.

City Secretary or Clerk. State law and city charters typically specify a City Secretary (Clerk) who is tasked with keeping the official papers and minutes of the City Council and managing other administrative details of the City Council office. Sometimes she is also tasked with other duties such as managing the business licensing function of the city. Like the City Attorney, the City Secretary is typically a "charter officer" who either works directly for the City Council or may serve the City Council by reporting through the City Manager.

City Auditor. Many, but not all, cities have a City Auditor who, like the City Attorney and City Secretary, is a charter officer. In nearly all cases, the City Auditor reports directly to the City Council. The City Auditor's duty is to provide an independent review of programs and policies to assure

City Council that their directives are being complied with. Typically, the City Auditor receives direction from an Audit Committee composed of members of the City Council and reports directly to the whole City Council. The City Auditor's focus is on compliance with city policy and law and his work is separate from the independent outside financial audit required at the end of each fiscal year. The City Auditor will create findings from his audits and make recommendations the City Council for improvements. The City Manager is then responsible to the City Council for implementing the approved recommendations. In larger cities, the City Manager may have need to examine the efficiency of certain operations. This is typically outside of the scope of the City Auditor's duties and may require the City Manager to appoint separate performance auditors that report directly to the City Manager.

City Manager. In the Council-Manager form of government, the City Manager is the Chief Executive Officer of the city. All the city's operations fall under the responsibility of the City Manager. The City Manager is responsible directly to the City Council for the performance of those duties, as outlined in this book.

City Council. This is the elected body to whom the City Manager, City Judge, City Auditor and, possibly, the City Attorney and City Secretary report. The primary responsibility of the City Council is to make policy and, through that policy, create the boundaries for decision-making within the organization. The City Council also must work within boundaries set by state law, charter, and their own policy. One of those parameters typically is that they must act as a body and cannot interfere in the operations of the city by individually giving orders or directions to any subordinate of the City Manager or by ordering the hiring or firing of any employee. The City Council is responsible to the electorate for the performance of their duties.

Although the foregoing is not a comprehensive list, it represents most of the things that cities do. The services provided by a city are very practical and basic to the every-day lives of the people who live in them.

Let's move on now and talk about the process of managing; the process by which City Managers handle the business of the city; the process by which they control for a desired outcome; the process by which they get the job done.

The management process

Cities are engaged is a mass of work as reviewed in the previous section. That work is disparate and too often unfocused. Unlike a private business, a city lacks the profit motive that often gives clarity to actions that must be taken. It is service oriented. It is public, meaning that it is constantly judged by people who have limited scope of details and high expectations. It is governed by a multi-person City Council who bring a variety of views as to what should be done and how the City Manager should do it. How does one go about managing this type of work under these circumstances?

When I was in graduate school, I was required to memorize several steps in the, then understood, management process. It went something like this: plan, organize staff, train, lead, direct, motivate and control. I have since developed a variant of my own regarding the theory of how management works. I have come to believe that managing pretty much anything uses the same process, whether it is a city, a private business or any other organization. The process is deceptively simple. Simple, like running a marathon: start running at the beginning of the race and keep running until you finish. It is not easy, however, because it requires much discipline, conditioning, mental preparation, endurance, and strategizing.

The management process includes three stages:

1. Evaluation.
2. Planning.
3. Execution.

Master these three stages and you will be good at the management process. Let's take them one at a time for a closer look:

1. Evaluation

The first thing you need to do is take stock of where you are compared with where you want to be. This may be a very simple and informal process as you begin, or it may be rather involved, especially after you have developed a track record of performance. Making an evaluation is always the first step.

I was once asked in a job interview what I envisioned my first days on the job to look like. My response was that I anticipated the first month would be spent getting acquainted with people and issues. While I believe that I am a quick study, I have learned that it takes a lot longer than a month to understand the people and issues within an organization, even when you know what you're looking for. Without clearly knowing it at the time, that entire initial process was an evaluation.

Almost always a City Manager will start a new job in the middle of someone else's budget cycle. That budget cycle may be amended a little, but not much. The inherited budget needs to be executed. During the execution, an initial evaluation will naturally take place and it will be of great assistance as you plan for the next budget cycle.

2. Planning

Following the initial evaluation phase, the planning phase comes next (See Figure 2). This is the process of thinking ahead, projecting and anticipating. It is about being intentional rather than haphazard. It foreshadows continuous improvement. It includes answering basic questions such as this: What are we going to do? What are the priorities? How are we going to do it? How will we pay for it? Who will do it? When will it get done?

When you think about it, these are very deep questions, even though they are very basic. When you consider the mass and variety of work a city does, it's hard to imagine that all the information and forethought for the whole city could fit into one document. In fact, it can't. So, the planning phase of city management is a multi-phase process. Please refer to the diagram to see a visual representation of what that process looks like and how each phase relates to the other. Let me cover each of the phases one at a time.

Comprehensive Plan. This is the big-picture plan for the city. It is the centerpiece of the planning process and generally has about a 20-year planning horizon. Everything that happens in a city should be foreshadowed or authorized in the Comprehensive Plan. Unfortunately, that is not the case in most cities. For most, the comprehensive plan is only a land-use document; it stops there. I advocate for a Comprehensive Plan that includes not only land use, but also functions as a controlling document for everything else that happens in a city. In other words, the Comprehensive Plan should truly be comprehensive and cover all aspects of the city. I will explain in more detail how the Comprehensive Plan serves as:

1. As a Controlling Land-use Document. The purpose of controlling land-use in a city is to protect all property owners and empower orderly development. Since

every parcel of land has a neighboring parcel of land, the intent of land-use control is to maximize the use while protecting all properties against neighboring uses that would devalue them. Land-use control not only protects the adjacent properties, but it also defines and protects the community. Questions such as these are answered in the Comprehensive Plan: How will the city protect the values and rights of all property owners? What limitations and allowances will there be on the use of any given parcel of property? How will the city grow? What will the city physically look like? Where will the major roads and thoroughfares be located? Where will the city parks be located? Where will utilities be located? These, and many other such questions are answered by the Comprehensive Plan. This part of the Comprehensive Plan will inform and spawn subsidiary maps, plans and codes, such as this:

- Future Land Use Map. A Future Land-use Map (FLUM) identifies where various zones of land-use will be within a city. Zoning must be compatible with the FLUM and provides more specific uses for specific parcels of land.
- Zoning Map and Zoning Code. Based on the Comprehensive Plan, Cities have both maps and codes that describe various land uses. The maps are a visual representation of the various zones, usually represented by different colors. The Zoning Code is a law which describes in written detail the various zones, their uses and restrictions.
- Development Codes. These legal Codes describe the process and requirements for developing property. Some Development

Codes are consolidated, with all requirements located in one chapter of the law. Other Codes are dispersed throughout the city's Code book. Included in these Codes are the requirements for developers to build public infrastructure and dedicate it to the city for perpetual maintenance.

- <u>Building Codes.</u> These Codes govern how structures are built and to what standards. They include codes for residential and commercial construction, electrical, plumbing, mechanical, fire and energy. Structures built in American cities must typically conform to these building codes. Some rural counties do not control building in the same way that cities do.

- <u>Property Maintenance Code.</u> Once a structure is built and a neighborhood is established, the Property Maintenance Code controls how it is maintained to remain safe and to uphold the property values of neighboring properties.

2. <u>As a Controlling Capital Improvements Document.</u> There is a natural flow from Land Use to Capital Improvements because, as you consider where and how the city will grow and develop, you must think about what public infrastructure will be needed to support that growth. When I say, "Public Infrastructure," I mean roads, bridges, airports, storm water pipes, channels and detention ponds, parks, trails, open spaces, recreation facilities, solid waste landfills and transfer stations, water lines, water storage tanks, water treatment facilities, sewer lines, sewer lift stations, sewer treatment plants, service yards and buildings of various sizes and purposes.

Questions such as these need to be answered by the Comprehensive Plan: Where will the water come from; how will it be transported; how will it be stored? What types of roads will be needed; where will they be located? These and many more such questions need to be thought about and answered. This part of the Comprehensive Plan will inform and spawn subsidiary plans, such as this:

- <u>Master Plans.</u> Master Plans take the infrastructure concepts from the Comprehensive Plan and work them into more applicable detail. These plans typically have about a five-year planning horizon. Individual Master Plans are typically created for:
    o Streets and supporting infrastructure.
    o Water
    o Sewer
    o Stormwater
    o Facilities and Buildings
    o Technology
    o Parks and Open Spaces
    o Major Vehicles and Equipment
- <u>Capital Improvements Plan.</u> Once the Master Plans are completed, there will always be more to do than resources will allow. So, the requirements therein must be prioritized and programed for construction, then matched up with available resources. The Capital Improvements Plan (CIP) is the document where this is done. The planning horizon for the typical CIP is five years, with a section for needed but unfunded projects. Projects will move from out years to near years as money

becomes available and is programmed to build them.

- Capital Budget. The first-year priorities from the CIP will move from the CIP to the Capital Budget. The Capital Budget becomes part of the city's Annual Budget.

3. As a Controlling Service Document. What types and quantities of service does the city want to provide its residents? What service expectations should the people have of their city government? How will the city deal with the five primary service areas: Public Works, Public Safety, Recreation, Community and Economic Development, and Support Services? How will services be paid for? What are the expectations regarding the nine management systems described in the next section? Most Comprehensive Plans that I'm aware of do not address the service levels that a community expects to receive, but they should. Without service clarity defined in a major policy document such as the Comprehensive Plan, the city is seriously in danger of mission creep; new services could be unintentionally added, or important ones could be minimized. Intentional decision-making and clarity in the Comprehensive Plan will minimize this problem. The Services part of the Comprehensive Plan will inform the Service Goals, and it will spawn more detailed operating plans, as follows:

- City's Operating Strategic Plan. After receiving its overarching goals and purpose from the Comprehensive Plan, the Strategic Plan prioritizes the goals and determines how to apply resources to the priorities. It answers questions about how the goals and targets of the Comprehensive Plan will be achieved. Each Department of the city should have a Strategic Plan with a five-year planning horizon. The combination of all the Departmental Strategic Plans makes up the city's Operational Strategic Plan. Key elements of the Operations Strategic Plan should include:

- o Stating the core values of the organization.
- o Being clear about the mission, along with articulating clear and simple definitions of the elements of the mission – mission elements.
- o Articulating the pinnacle issues. An environmental scan which identifies current conditions that affect implementation of the mission, predicted conditions and a Strengths, Weaknesses, Opportunities and Threats (SWOT) analysis can be helpful.
- o Identifying primary customers and those who will receive the service.
- o Articulating the priorities of each mission element.
- o Articulating strategies to achieve the priorities.
- o Identifying generalized costs of the strategies.
- o Identifying how the Operations Strategic Plan will be sustained in future years.

- <u>Annual Plan of Work.</u> The Annual Plan of Work will take the priorities from the city's Operating Strategic Plan and amplify them with details. The details include clarifying goals for each mission element. The goals should clearly state what will be done, who will do it, and when it will be accomplished. Longer-term goals should have interim targets. The information can then be placed into a database program, for both clarity and accountability, which can be regularly reviewed and managed.
- <u>Operating Budget.</u> The priorities of the Annual Plan of Work and costs of those priorities is then placed into the city's Annual Operating Budget. The Operating Budget becomes part of the Annual City Budget.
  - o <u>A Note</u> on the <u>Importance of Mission.</u> Each department of the city has a mission. Each mission can be divided into elements. For example, the mission of the Water Department is to deliver safe potable water to the community. Mission elements may include a) acquisition of future water supply, b) transportation of raw water, c) treatment of raw water, d) distribution of treated water and e) the business process of selling water and collecting revenue. Every Department will be similarly broken down by its mission into its mission

elements. The importance of mission cannot be overemphasized.

Each mission element will have goals and objectives assigned to it that make up the work of the Department. That work must be executed. The plan and the execution of the plan form the foundation of a performance measurement and reporting system, to be talked about later. All the goals, objectives and reporting will be directly related to the stated and clear mission of the department.

The first city in which I used this process, took more than one year to define and get clarity on all the missions of the various departments. In the second city, it took a little less time than that because the city was a little smaller and my previous experience in helped me be more efficient. In both cases, once the missions had been defined, they could not be changed without my consent because 1) being crystal clear on what you are supposed to do is vital; 2) incremental expansion of tasks and responsibilities, mission creep, is a very real, costly, and staff demanding issue in cities; and 3) the Plan of Work, Budget, and Performance Measurement Systems are all built on the firm foundation of Mission. Mission is vital.

Some cities create a mission statement in isolation of the management system. Boo!!! That is shortsighted and substantively ineffective. Those types of cities generally use flowery language and "poetry" to express their missions. I am totally opposed to poetry and flowery language in mission statements because it detracts from the primary purpose of giving crystal clarity to what the organization does and, by inference, what it will not do. Clear Mission provides a foundation for the entire management system through mirror images (See below.).

Another advantage of planning and executing the city's work by mission element is that rational decisions can be better made about increasing or decreasing services. For example, if the City Council wants to see more traffic enforcement in the Police Department (a mission element), the goals and performance of that mission element can be completely understood; new resources can be added or old resources can be shifted. When shifted, the impact on the area being shifted away from can also be better understood.

- Functional Mirror Images. What is a mirror image? It is when one component of the management system has the same format and structure as a companion component of the management system. For example, the budgeting system should have the same accounting codes and format as the accounting system; they should be mirror images. Not only should the budget be a mirror image of the accounting system, but it should also be a mirror image of the Annual Plan of Work. The Plan of Work should be a mirror image of both the Planning System and the Performance Measurement and Reporting system. The Planning System, the Plan of Work, the Accounting System, the Budgeting System, the Performance Measurement and Reporting System should each be mirror images of the city's Mission and Mission Elements. When complete, it should all fold together like an accordion.

Most municipal management systems have not been set up this way. To do so requires reformatting the accounting and budgeting systems and creating new systems for the other components of the management system. It takes a lot of time and energy to set up this sort of management system but it's worth it.

Annual City Budget. The Annual Budget is the financial plan for the next year which empowers and operationalizes the Annual Plan of Work. It is comprised of the Capital Budget and the Operating Budget.

Not all Cities keep their Capital and Operating budgets separated. It does makes good sense to do so because 1) many capital projects require more than one year to complete while an operating budget closes at the end of each fiscal year and 2) keeping track of capital and operating separately allows better analysis and control of each. Without separating them it is impossible to track trends in Operations spending.

In the real world, there is never enough money to do everything you want to do and usually not enough to do what you should do. It is impossible, therefore, to get a perfect match between the Annual Plan of Work and the Annual City Budget at the beginning. How I like to handle that is to make a draft Annual Plan of Work to begin with. On a staff level, match the budget and available resources to it. The draft budget is then presented to the City Council for public debate and ultimate adoption. Once the Annual City Budget is adopted, a revised and final Annual Plan of Work is created to perfectly align with the budget resources approved by the City Council. That is why the diagram in Figure 2 shows arrows going in both directions on the Annual City Budget.

In the functional world of City Management, a great deal of emphasis is placed on the Annual Budget. This is probably because it is 1) complicated, 2) mysterious, 3) it requires a lot of work by staff and Council alike, 4) there is much public process required of a budget and 5) it is required by law whereas other components of the management process are not.

This, however, is a very important point: The Budget should not exist in isolation of the work it empowers. It is not an entity unto itself. The Budget exits only to provide financial resources to accomplish the work that needs to be done. Of equal importance to the Budget is the Annual Plan of Work, which is a plan of what the money will be used to accomplish. The Annual Plan of Work and the Budget are complimentary, companion documents. I regret that, while all cities have budgets, only a few have Annual Plans of Work to accompany them.

Community Strategic Plan. A Community Strategic Plan (CSP) is a "big picture" document. It is bigger than the municipal corporation. It includes all other stakeholders in the community. It looks at the world in which the city, schools, businesses, non-profit organizations, and all other stakeholders that make up a community are nested. It considers all the factors that affect the community and identifies its overarching goals. It projects trends, identifies pinnacle issues and considers alternative application strategies. It prioritizes the issues and chooses between many alternatives to shape the community's future. If a CSP exists, it can be informative for the city to include some of its elements in the Comprehensive Plan. While it may be helpful, desirable even, a CSP is not required for a city to move forward with its management process.

One of the first and biggest questions to be asked when a community wants a CSP is, who should lead the effort? I have seen Chambers of Commerce do it; I have seen universities do it; I have seen private consultants do it; and I have seen cities make the attempt. In my opinion, none of them has done a very good job. Perhaps it's because they do not have a clear vision of what a CSP is; perhaps it's because building consensus around the future is close to impossible and there is no authoritative decision-maker in the community group. Usually, the effort devolves into a task list for the city to carry out rather than a truly strategic guiding document for all stakeholders in the community to put effort and resources behind.

In the Ideal World. It took most of my career to figure this stuff out. So, even though I understand this process well now, and even though I tried hard in my last two cities to achieve it, I have never worked in a city that had a fully populated planning model. It takes a lot of time, energy, coordination and cooperation to make it happen. It is the "ideal" condition to be striving for.

If we lived in an ideal world, the municipal planning process would work from top to bottom on the diagram (See Figure 2 on page 166); it would go from big picture to small picture in detail. The city's Comprehensive Plan would be the big picture, controlling document for everything that happens in the city. One phase would follow the previous phase and get increasingly detailed as it went along. Unfortunately, we do not live in the ideal world. We live in the real world and in most, if not all cities, it doesn't work that way. At least, I've never been in a city that had a complete planning model, and I don't know of a city that does.

Because cities are always required to adopt annual budgets, they will always have at least that part of the planning model. They may have nothing else. In those cases, the planning process is incomplete. It will still function, just not as well informed or as intentional or as efficiently as it otherwise could. Those managers who believe they can manage anything through their intuition, good judgement and good luck will continue to "wing it." Those who know what they are doing will not rest until the entire planning model is fully populated because they understand how important planning is to the process of management and how one municipal plan informs the next level of detail. Without a complete planning model, you cannot honestly answer the basic questions about what, when and how your organization is going to function; you cannot fully inform your internal leaders or the constituency; you cannot properly lead the organization; you cannot delegate the way you should; you cannot effectively measure performance against a pre-understood standard; you cannot fairly hold people accountable; the City Council cannot govern the way it should; and the city cannot excel.

Repeating, in the ideal world the planning model works from top to bottom. In the real world, it will work from bottom to top, until the model is completely populated.

3. Execution

Execution means carrying out your plan. Once your work has been planned, the plan must be worked (See Figure 3). Execution is getting things done. Getting things done is the ultimate reason why City Managers are a necessary part of city government. A City Manager who can't get things done is worthless. There are many techniques and tricks to the management trade, but I have found that there are two key execution principles bigger than all the others, and they are Clarity and Accountability.

Clarity. Clarity is just what it sounds like. It is removing ambiguity. It is having a full understanding of what is expected. For the boss, it is being able to answer the question, what is it exactly I want my subordinate to do? Write it down. When the subordinate has accomplished it, you should recognize, celebrate and reward. For the subordinate, it is being able to read what the boss wrote and know exactly what you must do to meet those expectations.

After the plan is in place, you will be able to answer the question, what are we going to do? Then, you must answer the next question: Who will do it? Once identified and assigned, that person will help answer the questions about how will it be done and when it will be done? Of course, there will likely be some negotiation, and then agreement, between the assigned party and the City Manager. In the end, the primary questions will be answered, and all of this leads to clarity.

In one particular city that I served, there was a great deal of work that needed to be done to institute change for improvement. A few departments were disastrous and needed serious change. For those departments, I put a lot of energy into being very clear and precise about what I wanted to see happen. Once I knew what would satisfy me, I was able to have meaningful conversation with the Department Head, or a potential new Department Head, about what needed to be done and whether they could accomplish it. We were both very clear about what was expected. In a few cases, I needed to find a new Department Head. But once done, I was never disappointed with the results.

Clarity leads to accountability.

Accountability. Accountability is the ability to hold someone responsible for doing something.

Inside of the Annual Plan of Work are scores of goals and many more performance targets. When compiled, there will be thousands of individual tasks. Each one should have a person identified as the responsible party to ensure it gets done on the agreed-upon timeline.

As I developed this system of management, I used a basic database program to manage these goals, performance targets and tasks. The database can be sorted by due date and managed by exception for those who may not be meeting their targets. I assigned an Administrative Assistant to manage the database. That person would notify me of any task that was off schedule and left uncorrected by the assigned executive. Typically, it did not take much of a conversation from me to get the work of the city back on track. Once people knew we were serious about executing the plan and that we were serious about accountability, things went very well.

This system is simple and very effective. There may be other ways of achieving accountability, but this is the best one I found.

Another dimension of accountability is regular reporting on the work achieved. With a system like the one I've described here; it is relatively easy to show and report on both progress and achievement. Providing regular reports on the status of performance is a great motivator for accountability. Additionally, it helps justify positive recognition and performance rewards.

In my opinion, the Employee Performance Appraisal system in a city should be based off the accomplishment of the Annual Plan of Work. In other words, the Employee Performance Appraisal System should be linked to the Annual Plan of Work. They should be mirror images of each other. All too often, performance appraisal systems are arbitrary, based on subjective criteria, and degenerate to an evaluation of personality. Real accountability and evaluation of performance should be primarily related to the accomplishment of the assigned work.

For the City Manager, providing regular achievement reports to the City Council gives them a very good sense of the work being done throughout the enterprise and it creates a system of accountability for the City Manager as well. It helps them exercise leadership among their constituency by helping them provide information. It helps them evaluate the performance of the City Manager and of the enterprise. I have previously indicated how I reported achievements and upcoming goals to the City Council on a 100-day basis. It was a very effective process for me and for the City Council.

<u>Performance Measurement and Reporting.</u> This is an important part of accountability. Intuitively City Managers know they should be measuring their work, but few know how to do it effectively. At one of the last conferences I attended, I went to a special workshop on performance management. It wasn't the first such workshop I had attended. They had worked hard to gather examples of many hundreds of performance measures. I asked the instructor how to know which of the many measures to use. His answer was to look over the list and pick the ones I liked the best. To say the least, I was very disappointed in the answer. In my opinion and experience, performance measures must be inseparably connected to the Annual Plan of Work; the Annual Plan of Work must be inseparably connected to the city's mission. Measurements without mission are meaningless. They become nothing more than busy-work.

The planning phase of the management process that I have previously described takes care of getting the mission and mission elements done correctly. The Annual Plan of Work takes care of identifying tasks and goals that are mission focused. These tasks and goals become the performance measures that have meaning to the organization and should form the basis of your city's Performance Measurement System. Of course, the performance measurement system is the mirror image of the Performance Reporting System. The Performance Reporting System becomes the instrument by which you can make both internal and external comparison of your performance. Using these comparisons forms the basis for the next cycle's performance and continuous improvement goals. Performance reporting is not only an important part of Execution, but it leads back to Evaluation.

4. Evaluation, again

Having completed the three steps in the management process, the fourth takes you back to the point of beginning where the process begins again.

The primary goal behind Evaluation is improvement, continuous improvement to the organization's ability to deliver service (See Figure 4). Evaluation is done by 1) comparing current performance to internal goals, 2) comparing current performance to external benchmarks and 3) conducting performance audits to discover weakness in process. The comparison must be accompanied with serious questions in mind: Why did we not meet our goals? Is there anything we can change to improve? Is there any other city doing this better than we are? If so, what are they doing differently than we are? Let's explain the three areas of comparison a little better:

Comparing to Internal Goals. There may be various ways to establish performance goals for the organization. The one I like best is to create an Annual Plan of Work for the city at the beginning of the fiscal year. The Plan of Work can be put together with the annual budget. The annual budget cycle, then, becomes the basis for performance evaluation. The Annual Plan of Work should contain performance goals for each mission element of the city. Those goals will most likely be founded on past accomplishment. Missing or exceeding that target will give cause to ask, why? That leads to "How?" The answers to those two questions will lead to intentional improvement.

<u>Comparing to External Benchmarks.</u> I'm a big proponent of comparing my city to others. The point is to look for another city that is doing a better job at one of the city's mission elements. Once found, the "Why?" and "How?" questions kick in. By learning how the other city does a better job, I can then go back to my own operation, innovate and make changes for improvement.

Before these types of comparisons and improvements can be made, you must know your own mission, mission elements and performance measures. Without this, proper comparison cannot be made. Also, since most cities don't think or manage like this, it may be difficult to find benchmarking partners who can provide valuable data because you will need to translate their data into your format.

Another consideration is that, in most cases, data needs to be normalized to be compared between cities. Normalized means comparing it to a common standard, like population or cost or time; for example, unit of performance per 1,000 population, unit of performance per $ or unit of performance per minute.

These types of external, mission-focused comparisons can be extraordinarily valuable to evaluating and improving the performance of your organization.

<u>Conducting Performance Audits.</u> Sometimes, the word "audit" carries a negative connotation. I don't mean it in a negative way. Perhaps "Review" or "Analysis" would be better words. The idea here is to analyze work processes to 1) make them more efficient and 2) look for ways to get to the end product smarter, faster, cheaper and with higher levels of customer satisfaction. There are several ways this can happen:

- City Auditor. Most cities, larger ones for sure, have City Auditors. Most of them work directly for the City Council; some of them work for the City Manager; it just depends on the specifics of the City charter. The Auditor's job deals mostly with looking for fraud and for compliance with City policy. Sometimes, the Auditor can be asked to look for efficiencies in the operation. Regardless of the specific tasking, the Auditor will review specific operations within the city government and, as a direct or indirect result of the Auditor's work, both problems and recommendations will be identified. The findings and recommendations are always presented to Management for review and comment. Those recommendations are very important for continuous improvement to the organization. The smart City Manager will take them seriously and make sure something good comes out of every recommendation.

- Continuous Improvement Team. Some cities do not have a City Auditor, or, in some cities, the Auditor is too busy to focus time and attention on the City Manager's priority areas. In those instances, I have found it very helpful, essential really, to form a continuous improvement team that is tasked with looking at priority areas of the city operation. Their mission is to find improvements in efficiency. The single most important tool I have seen these teams use is "process mapping." Process mapping commits to paper the very complicated steps in getting something done. By committing the process to paper and asking the question, "Why?", significant improvement can often be made. The most common answer people receive to the "Why?" question is because that's the way we've always done it. That, of course, is a totally unacceptable answer. Once the existing process is mapped, it can be dissected and recreated with new, more efficient steps. It is a simple, but magical process. There are other analytical tools that a continuous improvement team can use. The more experience they get, the better they will become at using a variety of tools.

- Departmental and Peer Reviews. Department heads do not, of course, need to wait for the City Manager to direct this process to occur to improve their departments. They can start their own improvement process within their department. In fact, I love it when a department head takes the initiative to evaluate the processes within his department and to take the steps necessary to really understand how the department operates and how it can be made more efficient.

    Sometimes these improvement efforts are undertaken by a department with the goal of justifying more employees. Wrong motivation! The purpose of continuous improvement is efficiency, not additional staffing. Advice to City Managers: don't let department heads misuse this important process.

    Some of the specialties in municipal services (for example: engineering, police or fire), are affiliated with state or national associations that provide peer reviews of their operations. Peer reviews consist of professionals from other cities working in the same specialty coming together to review a departmental operation against professional "Best Practices." While I have not generally found the peer reviews to be as helpful as the other types of reviews mentioned here for management purposes, they still have value and can be used to improve operations. Basically, they get a department ready for a deeper dive by one of the other methods.

Another variation of peer review is what I refer to as peer visits. It has always been surprising to me how much one can learn by visiting a neighboring or benchmark city. Cities, particularly cities that are underperforming, are very myopic. Employees do things without thinking it through because "that's the way we've always done it." Getting out to see how other cities perform the exact same mission can get the creative juices flowing and help departments re-evaluate how they are doing their work. And the other city is usually flattered by your interest in them, and they are quite willing to share what they know.

- Consultants. The use of subject matter experts to evaluate functions and departments can be very helpful for improving municipal operations. For example, if you wanted to evaluate the Information Technology Department, in most cases, internal people do not have the technical expertise or breadth of experience to do the evaluation. Trying to determine whether to have a fire-based Emergency Medical System or whether to contract that service to the private sector might require more independent expertise and experience than is contained within the municipality. These are but two real-life examples. In my experience, virtually every department and function can benefit from an outside review by experienced subject matter experts.

The process for using this type of evaluation tool is more complicated because of the municipal bidding or request for proposal requirements. Specifications must be written; bids and proposals must be evaluated and contracts must be negotiated and then approved by the City Council. It is much more formal. Managers must give a lot more advanced thought about the information needed from the study. To get the most helpful answers from this type of study, the right questions must be asked at the beginning. This requires hard and insightful work on the part of management.

One of the primary criticisms of this type of evaluation is that it will result in "one more study sitting on the shelf." Truly, City Managers must be careful to not let this criticism become a reality. One way I found to make sure a study never sits on a shelf is to require, as part of the study report, a prioritized list of recommended actions. I then take that list and build it into the measurable performance goals of the various departments. That way, people can be held accountable for getting the recommendations done and the study has great value and meaning.

The Management Process Is Circular, Not Linear

So, the management process contains three basic steps: Evaluation, Planning, and Execution. Rather than think of that as a linear process, it is better to think of it as circular (See figure 1.). Thinking of the management process as circular better represents the real world where we 1) get the important work of the city done and 2) create a culture of continuous improvement. Think about it; do you ever really plan something that you haven't evaluated, even if only in a rudimentary way, first? No. Do you ever evaluate something that you haven't first executed in some fashion? No. So, where does that process begin and end? It doesn't. It is on-going. It is best to think of the steps in the process as a circle. You can enter the circle at any given point and be somewhere in the process. The three steps can even, sometimes, run concurrently. It is a circular process.

Managers who understand the management process can better make intentional decisions. Understanding the process facilitates strategy and change management. The end goal of all of this is continuous improvement to the organization.

Management Process

(Figure 1)

PLANNING MODEL
(Figure 2)

Community Strategic Plan
(20-year Horizon)

* Schools
* Business
* Industry
* Non-profits

Building & Development Codes

* FLUM
* Zoning
* Development Standards
* Building Codes
* Property Codes

Comprehensive Plan
(20-year Horizon)

* What is our mission?
* What are our goals?
* What services do we want?
* What infrastructure do we need?
* What should our City look like?
* How will we pay for it?

Capital Improvements Plan

Prioritize individual projects from all Master Plans

Infrastructure Master Plans
(5-year Horizon)

* Streets
* Water
* Sewer
* Storm
* Facilities
* Technology
* Parks & Open Space
* Large equipment

Operating Strategic Plan
(5-year Horizon)

* Public Works
* Public Safety
* Parks & Recreation
* Community & Economic Development
* Support Services

Annual Plan of Work
(1-year Horizon)

* Includes Capital & Operations
* What will be accomplished?
* What performance targets and measures?
* Who will do it?
* When?

Annual City Budget

* Operating
* Capital

EXECUTION MODEL
(Figure 3)

Departmental Operating Strategic Plan	Department Annual Plan of Work
Mission 　Mission Element 1 　Mission Element 2 　Mission Element 3	* Mission Element #1 * Goal 1 * Goal 2 * Goal 3
For Clarity	For Clarity

Do the Work	Create Database of Performance Expectations
	Goal #1 　What? 　Who? 　When?
For Accountability	For Clarity and Accountability

Weekly review of database to assess goal accomplishment. (Manage this by exception.)	Correct Deficiencies
For Accountability	For Accountability

Quarterly Report of Goal Accomplishment
For Accountability

EVALUATION MODEL
(Figure 4)

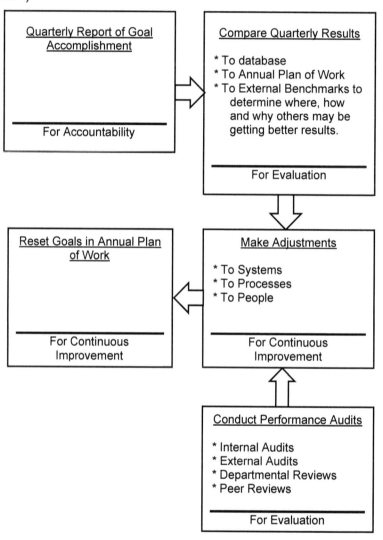

The Nine Systems

If one were to look at an organization chart of a city, they would see boxes connected with lines. Those boxes represent different entities, such as the City Council, the City Manager, and various Departments and Divisions within the city. The lines represent a relationship one box has with other boxes. Typically, if a box is below another box, it is subordinate to the higher box. If it is beside another box, it is generally equal with it. That type of standard organization chart does not adequately describe how those departments function and interact with each other. The boxes are very much interdependent rather than independent. Even the individual boxes representing departments are really systems of interacting people with interdependent responsibilities. This is true for the entire organization chart and especially true for the Support Services category of departments. The individual departments and all the departments working cross-departmentally form systems that are interdependent. For each of the other four categories of departments (Public Works, Public Safety, Recreation, and Community and Economic Development) to carry out their primary missions, they need support from the Nine Systems. Some of these Nine Systems are led by departments within the Support Services Group, but not all. None of the systems, even the ones led by Support Services, are independent because every Department of the city must be engaged with every one of the Nine Systems.

Some departments are bigger and better resourced than others. Therefore, some departments can oftentimes perform portions of the Nine Systems better than even the Support Services can. If they do, they will be duplicating service and wasting resources that belong to the entire city. Further, it is natural for individuals and departments to try to isolate themselves from the rest of the organization; they do it all the time. The City Manager cannot allow this to occur because it weakens the overall mission of the city and it destroys team efficiency. The city is the sum of its parts; it is a whole; it is an interdependent, interacting group of individual bodies; it is a system.

In addition to ensuring that the individual offices and departments on the organization chart are achieving their missions, the City Manager must ensure that these Nine Systems are working properly. Each of the Nine are subject to the Management Process, as are all the Departments and functions of the city. The Nine Systems are fundamental to and support all the service Departments in a city.

When starting a new job, the City Manager must evaluate these Nine Systems to determine how well they are functioning and interacting. The results of this evaluation will make up a significant part of the City Manager's agenda for managing and improving the organization. The Nine Systems are these:

1. The Governance System

Governance is the process by which the City Council exercises its governmental authority and control. The primary question is, how is that done? The answer: it is done through Policymaking. The City Council determines what the governing policy of the city will be. A policy is a clear, concise statement that gives direction for current and future action. Policy expresses the limits and restrictions of decision-making by other people. In other words, policy places boundaries on what decisions others may make.

One of the first questions a new City Manager should ask is to see the Governing Policies of the city. If the answer is given by referring you to the annual budget or the City Code book, that is an indication that there is a lot of work to be done on this system. While those documents are policy, they do not reflect a good system of policymaking.

What you should be looking for is a relatively thin book of policy statements that outline the City Council's statements regarding how they will, in fact, make policy, relate to each other, relate to the City Manager, and state the boundaries within which they expect the city to be managed.

The importance of having a clear and formal process for creating policy cannot be overstated. For a more detailed explanation, please refer to the previous section on advising the City Council, specifically the sections on policy.

Worthy of note again is the 3-D process I have described in other parts of this book. While making good, responsible policy decisions, follow the 3-D's: Discover, Debate, Decide. In that order. No variance.

The first of Nine Systems that the City Manager must ensure is working properly is the Governance System. It is the foundation for everything else that happens in a city. It must function properly.

2. The Management System

I have previously described the Management Process. The Management System is simply the way the Management Process is institutionalized in your city. So, making sure that 1) the entire Planning process is complete and populated with the full array of documents and all the thinking that backs up those documents; 2) the process for Executing the work is in place, along with the necessary training, technology and procedures and, 3) the process for Evaluating is in place, along with the necessary training, technology and procedures to make it successful. This will apply to all departments within the city.

3. The Money System

The money system includes the accounting, investing, purchasing, billing, petty cash, payroll, budgeting, and financial reporting systems. These systems must work together and, in many cases, must be mirror images of each other. These functions do not exist as "entities unto themselves" but rather to help with management decision-making, serving the department needs and to help meet overall management objectives.

4. The People System

The people system includes recruiting, testing, selecting, training, benefits administration, disciplinary support, risk management (although this function can be logically nested in any one of several other departments), job classification, compensation, administration of employee performance, collective bargaining or civil service administration and record keeping. Like the money system, these functions do not exist as "entities unto themselves" but rather to help with management decision-making, to serve the departments and to help meet overall management objectives.

5. The Technology System

The technology system includes network, applications support, and operations (the hardware such as desktop or mobile devices that run the applications for various departmental functions). Many people get lost in the technical jargon or operational complexity, but this system is central to all city services and is arguably one of the most important. This is one area that City Managers should not hesitate to bring in outside consulting help when it is needed to make sure that the technology systems are functioning as needed for the smooth accomplishment of the city mission. Like the other systems previously mentioned, these functions do not exist as "entities unto themselves" but rather to help with management decision-making, to serve the various department's needs, and to help meet overall management objectives.

6. The Customer Service System

Customer Service is very much an attitude. It's an attitude that should belong to every employee of the city. An organizational culture of Customer Service will always start at the top. Additionally, Customer Service should be a system with structure, parts and accountability. When someone calls the city regarding a service, the call should be logged in, action assigned to someone and follow-up made to ensure that the assignment was fulfilled. There should be supporting computer software to help manage the calls and there should be a work order system to make assignments and have follow-up to those assignments. I have always preferred a central call center. This, of course, works best in larger cities but the principle can be adapted to smaller cities as well. There should be a training component to Customer Service so that all employees know what is expected of them and how to act in relation to their customers. Lastly, customer service expectations should be written into every job description and made part of the annual performance evaluation. Like the other systems previously mentioned, these functions do not exist as "entities unto themselves" but rather to help with management decision-making, to serve the departments and to help meet overall management objectives.

7. The Communications System

Communication is critically important and includes website access, cable TV broadcasts of public meetings, creation of short "infomercials" that can be broadcast over cable or posted to a YouTube channel and in-person townhall-type meetings. Communication audiences include the residents of the community, employees, City Council members, prospective businesses and residents of the city. These various audiences may require a multitude of communication tools and techniques, including full use of social media. For those of us who have been in the profession for a while, the world has shifted, and we need to shift with it. Today's people demand more information and they demand it in the ways that best suit their lifestyles. We need to accommodate. Like the other systems previously mentioned, these functions do not exist as "entities unto themselves" but rather to help with management decision-making, to serve the departments and to help meet overall management objectives.

8. The Citizen Engagement System

Unlike communication which is a one-way process involving the city giving information to the people it serves, Engagement is an intentional two-way process that involves listening to and interacting with the people being served. Citizen Engagement might include things like regular neighborhood meetings or citizen academies. Citizen Engagement might include the use of social media, or it might be conducted in person. It may also include involving citizens in boards and commissions which give advice and counsel to the city leaders. Citizen Engagement should not be used simply to solve a current problem. It is more preventative in nature and allows city leaders and employees to listen to the needs of the "customer," anticipate their needs and be proactive. Like the other eight systems, this one also needs to be structured and methodical.

9. The Continuous Improvement System

Improving the operations of a city requires intentional effort and it is something that needs constant attention. I have previously described systems I have used. It is important to understand that creating a "system" for achieving these ends is vital to promoting a healthy organization. To be most effective, this effort must develop into a system that can be predictable and be, itself, subject to improvement. Systems for Continuous Improvement might include management review, internal or external performance auditing and the use of subject matter experts. Special skills training can be very helpful. Some cities even go to the extent of complex improvement systems like Six Sigma. That system works well in a manufacturing environment, but my personal experience with it is that it is more complex and refined than my organizations could use. Like the other systems previously mentioned, Continuous Improvement systems do not exist simply to be able to say we have them. They exist, rather, to help with management decision-making, to serve the departments, to help meet overall management objectives and to help them be the very best that they can be.

Experienced Insights

In the previous sections, I have explained the three-step process of management. That process can be adapted to any specific circumstance to meet unique requirements. What I'm going to cover next are several distinct topics inside of the management process that every City Manager will encounter while doing her job. Sometimes, because of unique circumstances, one of these topics will loom large enough to eclipse the management process, but keep in mind that these topics nest inside of the management process. They are always quite simply a single component of the overall responsibility to manage.

These are topics for which I have, from my experience, formed opinions on how to best apply the management process or I have developed techniques which have worked well. These special topics are as follows:

Budgeting

Budgeting is one of the very important pieces, but only a single piece, of the planning model previously discussed. I recall my first budget. I was so proud of that budget because it had taken SO much work; it was SO detailed and well documented, and it was BIG. And I assure you, I was the only one who understood that entire budget. Council Members asked specific questions about specific items that interested them to ensure they were included because they couldn't find them on their own. A few interested citizens asked questions, mostly about taxation, which I felt incredulous about because I didn't think they had a proper appreciation for the costs associated with public services or the amount of work that had gone into creating and balancing that document. Looking back, it wasn't a bad budget for the time or for someone fresh out of graduate school. It also wasn't a user-friendly one either; it wasn't the kind of budget that concludes a credible planning process or a budget that contributes to a coordinated management process.

I recall another budget where it was suggested that we do a "budget without numbers." It was a unique idea to me because prior to that, a budget was all about the numbers. When you think about it though, most people are not very interested in the numbers; they just want to know what the numbers will do. What services will they get, how much will it cost them? I learned a big lesson from that effort. Afterward, I applied my skill with numbers with the practical necessity of making the budget very understandable by focusing on what the budget was going to accomplish.

When I was in county government, I encountered a unique phenomenon that taught me more lessons. The politics were more pronounced, and half of the department heads were independently elected. The variety of presentation skill was extensive. Their reliance on political influence was also extensive and demanding. The Board of Supervisors firmly wanted to maintain financial integrity and financial control. To help address all these concerns, I developed a standard format for the budget presentations to the Board. The format was carefully thought through so that it contained a complete picture of each department: revenue and expense history, staffing, goals and objectives, projected issues, everything the Board needed to make an informed decision. Every department was required to follow the same format. At the end of each presentation, I made a recommendation to the Board. The Board understood the format and the budget because of the repetitive format, and they appreciated it. One of the department heads initially refused to comply with the format because she was an independently elected official and needed what was requested to run her office. The Board told her that, until she complied, they would not fund the department. Everyone finally got what they needed. I used a standard budget format for the rest of my career.

Later, I more fully explored the importance of mission and mission elements in relation to the budget. I began the process of aligning both the accounting system and budgeting system with the mission. Accountants will understand the magnitude of that effort because all the account code structure needed to be changed which can only happen in the short interval of changing from an old fiscal year to a new one. It was during that phase of my career that I began to manage the budget process more strategically. I moved from having departments prepare contingency budgets to telling departments what their budget target would be at the beginning of the process. This required a lot more work on the front end to project revenue and divide it strategically among the competing requirements within the organization. I created a budget "war room" where everything relating to the strategic direction of the city as well as the budget was laid out in charts and diagrams and posted on the walls. This saved a lot of work for departments and it allowed better strategic and policy control over the city's resources.

Throughout my career, I innovated and experimented with the budget process. I suppose that if I were still in the profession, I would still be innovating and learning new and better ways of getting the work done. As of my last budget, here's how I see it: The budget has three phases: 1) The Strategic Phase; 2) The Department Phase; and 3) The Public Phase. Further description follows:

<u>The Strategic Phase.</u> **This phase** belongs to executive management. In this phase, the City Manager relies on the fact that the previous planning products have been completed. In other words, there is a Comprehensive Plan. There is a Strategic Plan. There are the components of a Capital Improvements Plan. Those plans identify the strategic objectives and goals of the city. They have been adopted by the City Council and there is no need for special Council workshops to identify the priorities and goals of the City Council because they have already been expressed in the planning documents. The next thing to do is, as accurately as possible, identify the available resources. This is a difficult process because we are predicting at least 9 months in advance. Following the revenue forecasting, the City Manager must determine how those resources will be divided among the services, capital and debt service requirements of the city. Once that is determined, the various Departments Heads will be given the financial parameters within which to plan their budgets. Using this process will always result in a balanced budget with the least amount of duplicative effort. It will always address the city's most important priorities.

Some City Managers like to ask their departments to prepare three budgets, one that they think will be most likely, a second one on the contingency of having less money, and a third one on the contingency of having additional unanticipated resources. The City Manager then makes decisions on how to mix and match the three budgets into a final balanced budget. In my view, this type of process duplicates work, wastes a lot of staff time and doesn't really help the decision-making process.

For departments that cannot fit all that they want or need within the City Managers budget parameters, I ask them to prepare "decision packages." A decision package identifies a decision that could be made to add or change services within a department. It captures all the costs associated with that decision, including those costs that must be borne by other departments if the decision were made.

This process allows Department Heads to clear their conscience by identifying things they really need or want but could not fit into their budget parameters. If there are unanticipated resources available at the end of the process, or the decision package is important enough to shift resources between departments, it allows the City Manager to decide on where the highest priorities are for the municipal corporation. It is a very transparent process.

The Department Phase. This is what most people think of as the traditional budget process. It is where departments and the budget office crunch numbers, evaluate missions and priorities, and build an annual plan of work. This phase is largely invisible to the public and policy leaders, and it contains a gargantuan amount of work.

This phase includes presentations to the City Manager and executive team to educate, inform and flush out issues. It allows the City Manager to ensure that policies are being honored, priorities are being met and the attention to detail is sufficient to satisfy public scrutiny.

The last part of the Department Phase is to privately brief the City Council. This allows them time to begin to digest the mass of information prior to it becoming public. It does not shortcut or take anything away from the public phase. It simply gives the City Council a heads up on what to expect and it prepares them to answer immediate questions that they may face once the budget is publicly transmitted to them. This private briefing is for the City Manager to inform the City Council; it is not to get the City

Council's reaction or opinion or for the City Council to deliberate in any manner. This meeting is held with small groups of the City Council and "the rules of engagement" clearly posted on the wall so that neither the letter nor the spirit of the open meetings law is violated. Only clarifying questions may be asked by the City Council; they save all other questions for the public meeting. No opinionated comments may be made by the City Council; they save them for the public meeting. No deliberation may be done by the City Council; deliberation is for the public meeting. This is only a briefing. Period. I gave the exact same briefing to each of the City Council groups. I offered the exact same briefing to the press, on condition of their embargoing the information until after the public meeting.

A few additional observations are warranted here:

> The requirements of the open meetings laws are serious business and must be followed. It is not uncommon for the City Attorney to advise against briefings for small groups of the City Council. However, while the job of the City Attorney is to help keep the city out of legal trouble, it is also his job to counsel legal ways of doing the work. A simple "no" is not an acceptable answer without a recommendation of how to legally accomplish the will of the City Manager and City Council. If the City Attorney is resistant, a reminder is in order. If resistance continues, start thinking about new legal counsel. For the good of the city, City Managers must be able to communicate with their City Council, in both formal and informal ways. There are legal ways to accomplish this necessity. I know of one larger city that, for appearance's sake, has adopted a policy of not meeting in small groups or

communicating in any way outside of the formal City Council meetings. There has historically been a lot of contention in that city and the tenure of City Managers has been unusually short.

It is in the nature of many City Council Members to speak boldly and with authority on issues, to take strong positions. It comes with the personality type, and it comes with the job. As is often the case, if Council Members take public positions before they have all the facts, it is very difficult for them to change positions without being politically exposed or without being trapped into bad policy. Therefore private briefings on the most complicated and controversial topics are necessary for good policymaking. When they finally take a position, they will at least be in possession of all the facts.

It should be expected that the local press will push back on advanced small group briefings for the City Council. It has happened to me in every city where I've done it. You need to act within the boundaries of the law and they need to be reminded that you are doing so as well. You need to be very clear about the rules of Council and Staff behavior that will keep you within legal boundaries, and strictly follow them. Don't abuse the leeway or you will likely lose it. I also recommend that you invite the press to a briefing so that they know you're not trying to hide anything or break the rules and so that they are prepared with accurate information and good questions, as well. Even though you've had a private briefing, without deliberation, when the issue is brought into the public arena, make sure it is thoroughly and completely deliberated. The public has a right to know it all.

The Public Phase. After the other two phases are complete, the budget is publicly and formally transmitted to the City Council. This begins the Public Phase and allows the City Council to do their work in a very transparent way and it allows the interested public to learn the details of the budget.

A typical city budget contains hundreds, sometimes thousands, of pages of detail. It is very difficult for someone who has not been involved in the process to understand the complexity, structure and meaning of all the numbers in a budget. Consequently, I like to do more than simply hand the massive document over to the City Council. I like to summarize the material. It helps to think about the budget like a funnel. The top of the funnel is a summary of the highest level of information. As the information moves to the bottom of the funnel, it gets more detailed and specific. At the bottom of the funnel are the line-items for both anticipated expenditures and projected revenues.

In addition to simplifying the numbers by summarizing them and creating a "big picture," I like to make and standardize a presentation for each fund, department and major function of the city. Some department heads are more adept at making presentations and City Council members can be easily impressed by the presentation rather than the substance of the information. So, I have found that standardizing the presentation allows the City Council to get the information they need for the entire city and helps all department heads to adequately represent their mission, needs and proposed budget.

During the public hearings and public input phases, I have staff present a very high level, understandable summary of the budget so that credible, informed comments can be received. There are summaries for funds, major functions, and departments. The summaries include an explanation of mission, accomplishments, pinnacle issues, tables and graphs that represent staffing, department specific revenues and expenditures by major category. The final item in the summary is any explanation by the City Manager to help make the information or reasons for the decisions made in the proposed budget more understandable to the City Council.

The summaries are very important to Council and public understanding of the budget. It is not intended for the summaries to discourage or prevent anyone from looking at the budget in more detail. People are free to examine the budget material in as much detail as they like. This process simply recognizes that people cannot understand the budget by looking only at the detail. Numerous times, before using this budget process, I've had Council members or members of the public get their CPAs to examine the budget and try to explain it to them or tell them what questions to ask. While there is nothing wrong with that, even a private sector CPA can have difficulty mastering the numbers. The process I've explained here simplifies the budget and makes it much more understandable. It is a good way of doing a budget.

Change management

Instituting change in a city organization is a fundamental requirement. The entire concept of continuous improvement requires things to change. Poorly managed and/or poorly governed cities must be improved and that requires change. As I have tried to manage change in my cities, I have found the following actions to be most helpful. First, articulate a) legitimate reasons for change and b) a genuine sense of urgency. Second, articulate a vision for the result you wish to achieve. Third, form needed partnerships to support the desired change. Fourth, use the management process defined in this book to manage the change.[4]

My experience is that the first step is the hardest and the most important. You cannot manufacture an unreal reason or an illegitimate sense of urgency that will motivate people to lasting change. It must be a real reason and that reason must compel a sense of true urgency. People may act because the boss tells them to, but their actions will not be sustainable if that is the only reason for their action. An example of a real reason and urgency for change is this: Our organization is going to fail and cease to exist if we don't change the way in which we're doing business. Again, those statements must be truthful and well explained; they must be believed. If not, change will be temporary at best.

In addition to using this process for changing operational issues within the city, it can be used on other things as well. For example, I have observed many school district bond elections over the years. The successful ones very much follow the steps articulated here. Their urgency is related to the welfare of children, coalitions of parents and business partners are created, a vision of the benefits is promoted, etc.

I have previously talked about the Street Fee issue in Corpus Christi, mostly in relation to the 3-D process. The 3-D process was helpful to inform the City Council and public regarding a $1 billion backlog of street repair that was needed, which in turn created a sense of urgency. The rest of the change model came into play as the issue began to "get legs" and move toward a decision.

---

[4] For informative reading on change management, I recommend the works of Dr John P. Kotter.

100 Day Plans

Over the course of my career I found that getting things done required me to focus my attention and effort. It required me to limit what I was working on and try to not do too many things at once. If I could identify the most important thing and keep it as my only priority, I was most likely to get it done. Under no circumstances would I allow myself to take on more than three personal task priorities because the likelihood of getting more than that done was very low. Because a City Manager delegates much to subordinates, the same principle can be utilized with them. By delegating high priorities to subordinates a City Manager can get more than three things done for the enterprise, but the priorities of the subordinates need to be kept under three as well and they cannot all be the City Manager's priorities.[5]

Combining that principle with the sense of urgency that change management requires, I started using a system of 100-Day plans for myself. These plans contained the highest priority projects and change targets that I judged most important to the progress of the city. It is amazing how much can be accomplished when the focus is narrowed and urgency is created by setting a deadline, in this case the end of the 100-day period.

I first used this technique in Corpus Christi, Texas. The issues there were so numerous and so large that I could have easily become overwhelmed. Instead, after making an initial evaluation of the condition of the city, I broke my observations into categories and prioritized them. Knowing that my energy needed to be focused if I was going to accomplish anything at all, I put a small number of those priorities on a list with a 100-day target for getting them done. It worked so well for me that I did it again the next 100 days and continued doing it for the rest of my career.

---

[5] For informative reading on the topic of doing first things first, I recommend The 7 Habits of Highly Effective People by Dr Stephen R. Covey.

As City Manager, I controlled the priorities of the 100-Day Plan, but I shared my intent with the City Council at the beginning of the 100 days. I reported the outcome at the end of the period. It surprised me how much my City Councils appreciated those reports because it kept them informed. Many of them used the reports to talk to their constituents. Many of them kept the reports over time and then used them in my performance evaluation. The outcome of this process turned out to be far better than I initially imagined.

Taking Charge of Your Job

City Managers are like any other group of people. They come to the job with a variety of personalities and temperaments. One of the most important things a City Manager can do is get to know himself and get OK with it. If one is an extrovert, for example, you need to learn the positives and negatives of that personality type, minimize the downside and maximize the upside to get the most accomplished in your job and to get the most satisfaction out of it. The same goes for the introvert, and every other combination of personality and management style.

When you think about all the skills and abilities it takes to be a good City Manager, it is unrealistic to think you're going to be the best in all of them. There will always be associates who have better skills in one area or another. The goal should be to strive to have the best overall package of skills that are fit for the needs of a specific city.

Next, I would counsel the following: you shouldn't be shy about being in charge. Some City Managers are hesitant or look to the Council or to the Mayor to set their agenda or to give them permission to act. This is a big mistake because it promotes City Managers becoming caretakers rather than leaders. City Councils need City Managers who will take responsibility and act. They need their City Manager to be BOLD. I'm not talking about overbearing or rude or insensitive or un-participative. I'm talking about being responsibly bold. I'm talking about being unafraid to take on the hardest issues and unafraid to make the right decision, even if it is controversial. I'm talking about making sure that the City Council governs the way it should, and that City Managers manage the way they should.

Looking back on it, my leadership in some of my cities could have been bolder. I always had good support from my City Council and I could have used that support to help increase my boldness. It was a lesson I learned over time. The longer I was in the profession, the bolder I got. Further, I found that the cities that needed the most fixing required the boldest management.

Comparing that with my experience in Corpus Christi, Texas, there was a world of difference. The city was a mess when I got there. I went there because it was a mess; I wanted the challenge of fixing it. My family was grown, out of the house and on their own. My debts were minimal. My retirement was secure. All the factors that may have made me hesitant in the past no longer applied. I knew going in that change was needed and that making changes would require firm-minded action. In one of my first get-acquainted interviews with one of my Assistant City Managers, he advised, "When you see something that needs doing, just do it. Don't hesitate; don't defer." I already knew he was right. I fired people that needed to be fired. I reorganized departments that needed to be reorganized. I changed practices that needed changing. I publicly advised the City Council and told them the whole truth. I was bold in managing the city. And I was very successful at it. People recognized that I was trying to make a positive difference in the city. I carried the same attitude and bold management techniques into Killeen, Texas, for the same reasons I went to Corpus Christi, and it worked well there also. Looking back, I wish I had been bolder in all my cities.

Teambuilding

Another insight I have developed through experience is about teambuilding. While working together, department heads are like any other group of people. They will have disagreements and things will happen that someone does not like. It is natural for conditions to occur where one may prefer not working with another. It is also natural for competitive conditions to arise between some department heads. I have seen some City Managers who thrive on this type of drama and even encourage it in the hope that the competition will sharpen the performance of the individuals. This is the wrong approach. Cooperation, not competition, is the name of the game. A City Manager should always insist on cooperation and not tolerate anything other than playful competition between departments.

For this to happen, all department heads must understand the functioning of the municipal corporation and understand the importance of every other department. They must understand the mission, challenges and constraints of every department. When the team is working well, one department will voluntarily sacrifice part of its resource to balance out a weakness in another department. This takes a very mature organization. Department Heads must be willing to see and act beyond the borders of their own departments. City Managers must suppress ego and work for the good of the whole as well as the good of the individual.

Arriving at this condition is difficult. The City Manager must first envision it, train for it, then, eventually, insist upon it.

I have always used a team approach for putting the City Council agenda together, usually in the form of a staff meeting. Those staff meetings can become a form of training session. By using the agenda staff meetings for training, I could share my philosophy of leadership and management. We used the actual topics from the past City Council meeting as examples to dissect and discuss for the purpose of training and improvement. We rehearsed upcoming agenda items, along with peer feedback for improvement. When using the agenda staff meeting in this fashion, the City Manager should be cautious to not prescribe words, phrases or specific speaking characteristics on the subordinates. Each presenter needs the freedom to be himself or herself. There should be more coaching and little prescription. The kind of training and feedback I tried to engender was always intended to build, teach and improve individual skills while giving the presenter freedom of self-expression. It worked seamlessly well, and the City Councils often commented on the competence and professionalism of staff presentations. Many staff members thanked me for the training. In a similar fashion, we used the annual budget as a training opportunity. I required all Department Heads to attend the rehearsals for the final budget presentations, not so much for their individual coaching but for them to learn about the issues, challenges and constraints of their fellow departments. Again, I found Department Heads not only willing but anxious to attend because these were great learning opportunities for them. Many thanked me for that training as well.

Delegating

Delegating is a key to success in management leadership. The hardest part of delegating is getting past the notion that no one else can do the job as well as you can. That type of thinking makes it hard to give someone else an important assignment. It also creates a tendency to micromanage people while they fulfill the assignment. Just keep in mind, managers who cannot or will not delegate cannot be good managers. The essence of management is getting things done through other people.

A City Manager should spend a great deal of time thinking through and writing down exactly what the expectations are for the end result. Clearly communicating those expectation is vital to success in delegating.

Being available to assist and coach subordinates to successfully meet expectations is important. Recognizing good effort and good outcome is important. Coaching, teaching and developing others in a non-threatening, helpful way, rather than trying to control the details, is vital to a City Manager's success.

Trust

Trust is what makes the organization work and be successful. Period. End of story.[6]

When a community does not trust its city government, that government struggles to be successful. When workers do not trust their leaders, performance will be poor and the ability to create synergy will be greatly diminished. When one person does not trust another person, working relations will be strained.

To be trusted, a person must be believed. To be believed, one must tell the truth and keep her word, consistently, and repeatedly. Trust is built on ethical behavior. Ethical behavior is built upon being honest, fair, telling the truth, and keeping your word. It's that simple. To be trusted means that other people believe that you will do the right thing, the ethical thing, for the right reasons. Trust is proven under challenging conditions when it is difficult to do the right thing. Anyone can do the ethically right thing when the decisions are easy; not everyone can do it under stressful conditions.

What does one do when there has been a breach of trust? Let's face it, people are not perfect. Mistakes will be made. Trust will be broken. How do you fix it? The answer is this: return to the basics of ethical behavior. You can't erase the breach, but you can acknowledge it and apologize for it. Then you can begin again to act honestly, fairly, truthfully and with real intent. It will take time, and eventually trust can be restored. Broken trust is one of the characteristics of a broken, failing organization.

---

[6] For informative reading on the topic of organizational trust, I recommend The Speed of Trust: The One Thing that Changes Everything by Stephen M.R. Covey.

Trust is the most valuable commodity an individual or an organization has. Never sacrifice it for anything else that seems important in the short run. Sacrificing trust will destroy the long run.

As I just said, people are only human; mistakes will be made, and trust will be broken. So, how many breaches in the public trust can a city endure?

I recall an instance at a city golf course. It was a nationally ranked course. Golfers came from across the nation to play. The staff was professional and well liked. One day my office received a tip from a former, supposedly disgruntled, employee. The tip said that there was employee theft taking place in the clubhouse. I turned it over to the police to investigate, as I always did, because even when I had doubt about a complaint, I wanted to eliminate any possibility of allowing an illegal act to occur. A few days later the Police Chief reported back. He said they had investigated the matter and found indications that theft, indeed, had occurred, but it looked minor. He intended to offer legal immunity to one of the employees in return for an admission, information to do a more thorough investigation, and implication of anyone else involved. I concurred. A couple weeks later the Chief reported to me again. There were several employees involved in the theft, including the golf course manager. The size of the theft over two years was more than $100,000, much larger than anyone had originally anticipated. We fired all involved. We prosecuted those that didn't have immunity. The court ordered restitution of a portion of the stolen money. The press was not nice to us. Public trust was seriously damaged.

Lessons learned: When you run into fraud, you should always assume that it is bigger and deeper than you initially thought; it's always more than you can prove. So, never offer immunity too quickly. Make sure your financial systems are protected with layers of approval authority and set up to force illegal activity to require collusion. The more people that are required to collude in illegal activity, the less likely will be their success. There is no way to completely stop a determined thief, but you want to make it as difficult as possible and you want to be able to catch the theft as quickly as possible.

In another city, the Recreation Department had a division that was responsible for specific recreation services and facilities maintenance. One day, we received a tip from a former employee that theft was occurring in that division. We had recently established a government and white-collar crime unit in the police department. I turned it over to the Chief of Police to investigate. Sadly, they reported back that the allegations were true. We brought in a forensic audit team to investigate it. They found missing engines, ATVs, cameras, purchase of unnecessary equipment, and a phantom employee that we had been paying for a couple of years. The amount of the theft, that we could prove, was in the high six figures. The manager of that division corrupted the financial system by colluding with others to carry out the fraud. We fired and prosecuted the people involved. In this case, the court ordered full restitution, but the public trust damage was enormous. The director of the department was not involved in the theft, but he resigned anyway. I admit that management taking swift and decisive action on the problem helped, but the damage this sort of thing does to a city cannot be erased.

Such breaches are, of course, not limited to the public sector but in the public sector, they are always known and published. When such things happen, cities are damaged tremendously. Maintaining trust is vital.

Show Me

In relation to the nuclear disarmament treaty, President Ronald Reagan is famous for using the phrase, "Trust, but Verify." Following the Recreation Department fraud previously mentioned, I heard that phrase a lot from my staff as a part of their lessons learned. The phrase never seemed completely satisfactory to me because trusting people but verifying their work seemed contradictory. For me, a more accurate way of expressing the thought may be, trust your internal control systems and verify that they are working.

There is no substitute for good internal control systems. Systems are impersonal; they do not exercise judgement or have personal feelings of greed or ambition. Systems that are built on personalities rather than processes will eventually fail because people are flawed. Even the best people will eventually make mistakes and disappoint. That is not to say that people are bad, because they are not. They are just human. We are all gaining wisdom by learning from our mistakes.

One of the big realities for City Managers is to recognize that the public coffers and the public trust need to always be protected. So, my rule is: Set up good internal controls and audit them; realize that no system is perfect and neither is any person. Be prepared to deal with the failures of both.

Not long before my arrival in one of my cities, they had installed a new accounting software. My Assistant had been delegated the responsibility of overseeing the financial operations of the city. Every month, I asked him questions about the city's finances. The answers were always positive; everything is good. Toward the end of the fiscal year, my Assistant found a new job in another city. Good for him. With him gone, I needed to assume his duties for the financial operations. To my surprise, the new software was not functioning properly. The utility billing, accounts receivable, accounts payable, payroll, etc. had not been fully posted or reconciled for more than nine months. For a few hours, my mind was in a panic. I called our external auditors to see if they could help. They were sympathetic but unwilling to assist for an affordable price. They were auditors and their contract dealt with auditing the records at the end of the fiscal year, not doing the bookkeeping. To make a longer story short, we got the software glitch fixed. Then I assembled all the financial records of the city into a vacant room, organized them by date and type. Then, I hand entered every entry into the software. For each month, I reconciled the general ledger to the bank statements. I worked twelve-hour days for several weeks, including weekends. I finally got the system caught up. Disaster averted.

Lesson learned: Don't just tell me, show me.

The Art of City Management

There is a scientific, mechanical, hard side to city management. There is also the soft side of the profession. The soft side is the people side of the organization. It is in the soft side where the *art* of City Management makes its appearance. Human beings are totally unique and difficult to predict. The art of city management deals with the ability to anticipate, predict and prepare contingencies for the people side of the business. Although these soft skills may have been taught in Organization Behavior programs, or other fields when I was in graduate school, they were not taught in my MPA program. I suspect other MPA programs are similar. Some City Managers never have the art in sufficient quantity to succeed. Others have a "sixth sense" about being able to "read" people. The art applies to anticipating the City Council and predicting what they will do or understanding how the public or staff will act in certain situations. The art applies to one's ability to lead and motivate. The soft side of the organization requires a high level of intuition and interpersonal skill. I am not suggesting these skills be used for anything manipulative or underhanded, only the most honorable of intention and action. People who are not good at the art of City Management should consider staying in a technical or subordinate position in the municipal organization until their skill set is better developed.

Hiring People

The City Manager has only several direct reports in the organization. Typically, they are Assistant City Managers and

Department Heads. So, how does one select good, competent people? The recruitment and selection processes in cities are well defined. These processes must be public, transparent and equally open to all qualified persons. Therefore a great deal of thought should go into the initial description of duties and qualifications. After that, the field needs to be narrowed. This can be done either by the HR Department or by a consultant, depending on the organization needs and talent of the staff in the organization. In either case, through resume' screening, supplemental questionnaires and initial interviews, professionals can find technically qualified people to fit the jobs. Next comes the issues of organizational fit and personal ethics. These are the purview of the City Manager. I would argue that only the City Manager can make these two final decisions. As I have hired direct reports, the issue of their personal ethical values and their commitment to those values has become the primary decision point. Keep in mind this truism: every organization will ultimately begin to look like and take on the characteristics of its leader, be it a city or a department or a subdivision of a department. The ultimate success of the organization will hinge on the ethical values of the people. Ethical values will lead to trust. Trust will lead to success. Ethics is a hard thing to detect. The right questions need to be asked. Making a good hiring decision requires a well-developed sense of discernment and the exercise of the art of city management. Technical competence is important, but it is secondary when selecting executive leadership.

Firing People

Along with hiring people, the unpleasant responsibility to fire people also comes along with the job as City Manager. Employment in the public sector is quite different than employment in the private sector. Unlike the private sector where most people work "at will," with few exceptions, city employees have a property right to their employment. You cannot take away city employee's property (job) without due process. This means that you must have provable reasons and a fair process that allows an employee to explain and defend herself before she can be fired or deprived of her property. The City Manager needs to ensure that the rules and processes are in place and being followed regarding employees who have a property right to their positions.

Now, the exceptions to the property right rules are those high-level executives who work directly for the 'City Manager, and certain "confidential" employees who support them and are entrusted with confidential information. This group is considered to be "at-will." The City Manager should consult with an attorney to make sure that legal requirements are understood and being met before firing at-will employees. I have several observations and recommendations for this class of employee:

1. Before you fire someone, make sure you have been clear about your performance expectations and that you have given the person a fair chance to meet those expectations.
2. In coaching a subordinate, the City Manager should be candid and honest. Some managers try to put pressure on subordinates to encourage them to resign. This is cowardly, unprofessional and should never be done. If the person is willing to receive it, the most valuable gift that can be given is honest feedback. It is the only thing that will help a person correct performance or behavior that is substandard, move on with his life, and become successful in a different location. Unfortunately, from my experience, most people are not willing to receive that kind of hard feedback so most of the time it is withheld. By the way, if you're an employee in that circumstance, the best thing you can do for yourself is request the feedback and gratefully receive it for as the gift that it really is.

3. Working at the executive level of the organization means that higher expectations are placed on people in those positions. The rules and guidelines for separating people at this level are different than those who have a property right with their employment. Make sure you understand the laws before you proceed.

4. Most City Charters have language indicating that subordinates of the City Manager work at his/her pleasure and that they may be let go for the good of the service. After the coaching has failed, expectations are not being met and the City Manager loses confidence in an at-will employee, that is all the reasoning that is needed to initiate a separation. To avoid future litigation, that is the only reason that should be given, even though by that time the reasons are numerous.

5. When letting an executive go, it should be done with professionalism. It should be confidential. Assuming there has not been gross malfeasance, either a severance or a transition time should be given, allowing the executive to make a professional transition.

6. There may be occasions when a termination will come as a surprise to a subordinate, but such occasions should be rare. Reasons for the rare occasion may include a) a case where the position is highly sensitive and the person is likely to become angry, respond unprofessionally and do the city great harm; b) a situation where there is malfeasance or fraud that simply cannot be fixed with reasonable time or effort. When these exceptions occur, the City Manager should act swiftly and decisively to exit the individual from the organization.

Unions and Collective Bargaining

There was a time when membership in public sector unions was relatively low, certainly lower than in the private sector. That is no longer true. Since about 2009, membership in public sector unions has exceeded that of the private sector. This is an area of city management that threatens many City Managers, but it shouldn't.

Different states have varying attitudes toward unionization, and they have different laws governing how it works. It is good for City Managers to thoroughly understand the laws of the state in which they work. If you take a job in a union state and you are new to unions and collective bargaining, I suggest you get a crash course from your City Attorney or labor relations people. I also recommend getting affiliated with the National Public Employer Labor Relations Association (NPELRA) or at least getting some training from them. As with anything else, the more you know, the better you deal with it.

Once you have a contract with a union local, you simply need to abide by it. There is nothing a union can force you to do that is outside of the contract. They probably won't even try. Some people have the mistaken idea that, if you are unionized, you can't fire people who are doing a bad job. That's not true. The union contract will simply require that you go through a process to do what you need to do. Sometimes the process will be arduous. If so, you just need to persist through. One of the biggest problems I have observed is that public sector managers are not persistent enough. There are probably many reasons for that, but I'm not going to try to cover them here. Suffice it to say that City Managers need to be more firm-minded than they might otherwise be, when dealing with unions. You need to look out for the best interest of the city. I assure you that the union will look out for the best interest of its members. If those two interests converge, so much the better. Because it already happened, you need to get your head around the idea that someone before you will have agreed to provisions in the contract that you don't like. That's no reason to defer action. Live with the contract for now and change it later if you can. Every provision in a contract has value. To change a provision, you will need to trade its value for the value of something else.

If you don't have a contract to begin with, once a group of employees qualifies to unionize, you will need to negotiate one. Here are a couple of points to keep in mind as you do so:

1) You need to know the facts and your goals. You need to be prepared. I like to put together a negotiating loose-leaf binder that contains all the necessary information before the contract negotiation. If you don't know what that information should be, contact your labor relations expert.

2) You will need to keep your City Council fully informed all the way through the process. Contract negotiation strategy legally qualifies for a closed meeting in most states. Use that provision. Ask the City Council to consent to the negotiating goals and targets. Keep them informed on the progress toward achieving the goals and targets. Don't let the union outperform you in keeping the City Council informed. They will try. The worst thing that can happen is for the union to tell the City Council something before you do because it will seriously undermine the Council's confidence in you.

3) Be assured that the union has sympathetic friends on the City Council. The union has kept in close informal contact with Council members throughout the years before the contract expired. The union has probably contributed to Council members election campaigns, either monetarily or by volunteer workers. BUT know this: The City Council members have a serious fiduciary responsibility to look out for the taxpayers and it is illegal for them to disclose the city's negotiating strategy or goals. Doing so could place them in deep legal danger. Make sure they understand that.

4) You need to treat the union representatives as equals at the bargaining table, because they are.

5) While at the bargaining table, you don't need to agree to anything you consider unreasonable. If you can't agree, there will be a process for getting settlement. If you work in a union state, there will be rules and a process for mediation. There will be rules and a fair process for arbitration. At the end, you will have a contract. You may not like it, but neither will the other side. If you work in a right-to-work state, the rules and processes may not be as clear. There may or may not be a process that forces a conclusion to negotiations. If a process is in place, it will be like the one described previously, except there will be no state oversight. If there is no process, you will need to consult your labor relations expert to get guidance.

I have worked in two right-to-work states, Utah and Texas; two union states, Michigan and Ohio; and one state (Iowa) that was technically right-to-work but as a practical matter, at least in the county I worked in, was a union state. The principles of labor relations remain the same in all the states, and the details vary greatly. For what it's worth, I have found it much easier and better to work in union states, if you know what you're doing. I gained my working knowledge of labor relations in Michigan under the tutelage of an expert labor attorney and a labor advisor from the Michigan Municipal League. I will always be grateful for their instruction because it has helped me in every city I have managed since then.

Keeping an Emotional Distance from City Council Decisions.
City Managers and their staffs work hard on policy and ministerial issues as they prepare them for the City Council meetings. It is easy for them to form opinions and become passionate about what decisions the City Council should make

regarding them. This is a mistake. Deciding final outcomes is the job of the City Council. As much as staff resents City Councils interfering with staff work, City Councils should resent staff interfering with Policy work. A City Manager should always remember and teach the staff, that their job is to assist and advise the Council. This is accomplished by making sure that problems are well defined, facts are discovered, alternatives and costs identified, questions answered and when appropriate, recommendations made. Everything after that belongs to the City Council. The City Manager and staff need to do their job with excellence. They need to let the City Council do their job as they see fit. Getting emotionally involved with outcomes or trying to control outcomes is harmful to both groups. Further, keep in mind that City Councils and staff see the same issue from differing points of view. City Councils look at an issue and ask, how can we best serve and build the community? The answer may lead to compromises in standard procedure to satisfy the important needs of a portion of the community. Staff looks at the same issue and asks, how can we be consistent, do the most good for the least cost? The answer may lead to saying "no" to a small portion of the community. Both perspectives are good, and necessary to city decision-making. If the City Council makes a decision that staff doesn't agree with, they must console themselves with the fact that they did their job and so did the Council.

Total Cost Decision-making

Too often calculation of financial impacts is incomplete and shortsighted. Projecting costs is important to good decision-making. Let me give some examples of this.

Fleet. When calculating the cost of cars, trucks and other equipment, more than the initial purchase price should be considered. The cost of gas, oil, and other maintenance as well as salvage value should also be taken into consideration. Total cost over the life of the asset is a much better gauge of value than purchase price alone.

High Density Housing. Higher densities of housing require more parks, open space and recreation; more public safety services; and more public transit service than lower density zoning. I'm not trying to make a value judgement about which is more desirable; I'm just saying that the City Council deserves to have all the information before they make the decision.

Homelessness. For the most part, homeless shelters are run by non-profit organizations and, in many cases, are partly supported by city financial contributions. Shelters have a financial impact on the city through increased public safety requirements, possible depression of commerce and therefore reduction of tax base and higher impacts on medical services. One of the things we experienced in one of my cities was the shifting of the mission of the Public Library. Because of homeless shelter policy to prohibit persons from remaining in the shelter during the day, the Public Library became the de facto day shelter for the homeless. The library began to see much less of its originally intended purpose, while security costs went up and employee turnover costs increased. The total cost of decisions regarding homeless services should be considered before public money is allocated to support homeless shelters.

Public Transit. For most small to medium sized cities with transit systems, 90% of the operating costs are paid for by the federal government. Most cities think of it as a bargain because they are getting the service for 1/10th of the actual cost. I think the City Council should know the total cost before making decisions regarding the service.

Subsidized Housing. Cities have very little control over this service; there are significant impacts on Cities. Areas where subsidized housing is common experience higher demand for city services. Not only are city services impacted by subsidized housing, but the nature and climate of neighborhoods can be changed. Income levels change, which has a negative impact on the city's tax base. Significant businesses may relocate, partly based on those changes, again impacting employment and tax base.

Capital Projects. Capital projects are things such as roads, bridges, parks, and buildings. Those assets are usually paid for through borrowing. When making capital projects decisions, most all the attention is on the purchase price of the asset. Little thought is given to the costs of operating the asset, but it should be considered. When the City Council is deciding whether to borrow money for a capital project, the City Manager should ensure that the operating costs are also considered, and an allocation placed in the annual operating budget to cover those costs.

We had a circumstance in another city where a bond issue had been approved by the voters prior to my arrival in the city to construct a new fire station. At one point, the Fire Union began drawing attention to the fact that there was an approved fire station and the City Manager was holding up construction. (I think the standoff we were experiencing over the union contract may have had something to do with their timing.) I had to make it clear to the City Council, the public and the union that while we had bond money to build the new station, we did not have money to buy the fire apparatus, ambulance, hire 18 new staff and pay for annual maintenance costs on the facility. I wasn't holding the construction of the new fire station to harass the union; I was holding it because the total cost of the decision had not been considered at the time of the bond election. We didn't have enough money to execute the decision and it would have been a compounding error to build the station only to board it up for lack of resources to operate it.

These are all examples of total-cost decision-making. As you can see from the examples, some of the issues are politically and socially sensitive so they are often glossed over. I am not being critical of the social or political policy issues themselves. I am only pointing out that total impacts should be disclosed and considered before policymakers make decisions. The decisions are theirs to make. In my view, they need the information; do with it whatever they may. For political reasons, some politicians don't want the information; they want deniability. The City Manager should ensure that they get the information anyway because the downstream narrative will likely be that staff withheld information that would have changed their decision if they had known it.

Presentations

Developing presentation skills for both the City Manager and the staff is very important. This is a special form of communication that will get a lot of attention because 1) it is formal and very public and 2) the City Council relies on information presented to them to make good decisions and good policy. Not all Department Heads or Assistant City Managers, or City Managers for that matter, are born with good public speaking abilities or good presentation skills. They all need to be trained and they need to receive feedback from their colleagues. Training on presenting issues to the City Council should never stop, hence, the agenda rehearsal meetings for staff.

Following a City Council meeting, a gentleman approached me with some feedback regarding a presentation I had made to the City Council. After his feedback, he invited me to attend one of his seminars. He was a retired executive who had set up his own communications consulting business. He trained people to make effective presentations. I declined, thinking that I was being quite successful in my city and that he was just out to drum up business for his own profit. Over the next year or so, I declined several more invitations even though he offered the seminar to me without cost. Finally, I became weary of his persistence and accepted his invitation. It turned out to be some of the most impactful training I received during my career. He taught how to be concise, direct, and short in communicating through presentations. The effectiveness of his teaching was even further driven home when a loved ones passed away. Each of the speakers had received their communication training and each used their training in making remarks. It was one of the best (if that word can be used for such an occasion) funerals I have ever attended.

The training I received from this gentleman improved my career. It helped me clarify the purpose and process for making presentations. It altered my expectations of staff and outside presenters in City Council meetings. It added to my thoughts on staff training.

Under the proven influence of this training, here are the presentation guidelines that I developed over the years:

1) With proper preparation and practice, early every message can be delivered in less than three minutes; that should be the time target. In that time, the most important and memorable points can be made. I have been known to take a three-minute hourglass to rehearsal meetings. When the sand runs out, so does the presentation. It is good training. Of course, during the real presentation, I would never interrupt, but the point is this: short is best.

2) It takes practice to achieve that three-minute goal. Every presentation should be rehearsed.

3) PowerPoints are aids to your presentation; they are not the presentation itself. The spoken words are the

presentation. PowerPoint slides should never simply be read. It takes about one minute per slide to properly communicate what the slide is trying to convey; limit the number of slides in any given presentation to fit the timeframe allowed for that presentation.

4) Outside presenters will not have the same training as staff so they should be coached in advance and given up to 10 minutes to deliver their message. This needs to be controlled by staff because, trust me on this, outsiders will use much more time if they are allowed. If a preview of an outside presentation reveals that they are bringing 40 slides, you better get involved and amend the presentation. I assure you that the City Council will be bored to death after ten minutes and not hear a word said after that. Once they get used to good presentations, they will be cranky at the City Manager for allowing poor presentations to waste their time.

5) Focus on the top three points that need to be made. Never use acronyms or technical language. Use words that everyone can understand. Keep it direct and simple.

6) Don't try to anticipate and answer every question before it is asked. Time for questions is on top of the 3-minute limit. Let the City Council ask their questions.

Politics

It used to be that politics was the art of dealing with conflict and compromise. In today's world, I think it more accurate to say that politics is the exercise of power. In a city, that power is dispersed and exercised by elected officials, as a group, not as individuals. In Council-Manager cities, the Mayor is part of the City Council. When individual members of the City Council are allowed, by the Council itself, by the citizens, or by the City Manager, to exercise individual power, the governance of the city is going astray. A high price will ultimately be paid for the departure. The high price will come in the form of contention, disorder, poor decision-making, confusion, erosion of trust, lack of confidence, fuzzy vision, failed consensus-building and poor policy.

City Managers also exercise power in a city, but only that which is delegated to them by the City Council, the City Charter or other forms of governance law. Getting clarity about that delegation through charter, policy, formal motions of direction, ordinances and resolutions is vital to good order and to discourage the improper use of power. That delegation should be clear enough to place a boundary around the City Manager's decision-making authority and broad enough to allow the City Manager, as the city's Chief Executive Officer, to act and execute.

Another form of power is informal power. For example, information can be power. Because City Managers are usually privy to information before the members of the City Council, unethical and unprofessional City Managers can use that information to manipulate the outcome of decisions. In those cases, the City Council should quickly and decisively exercise its power to fire and replace that City Manager.

A less desirable definition of politics relates not to the use of power, but to the abuse of power through strategic manipulation and various forms of deception and dishonesty. City Councils are comprised of odd numbers of voting members, such as 5, 7, 9 or 11. This is so they can occasionally disagree as individuals and still have a majority to move the work of the city forward. Majority rule is a foundation principle of governance by democracy. However, when a City Council is consistently split, and working on a thin majority in their decisions, especially when they form teams and vote as a block, it shows an inability to build consensus and results in very weak policy.

Because the City Council members are inevitably going to disagree on things, this less desirable form of politics comes into play. It is human nature. I would be less than honest if I did not admit that it exists in City Government. This is the definition of politics that causes most elected officials to dislike being called a politician. It is this definition that causes people to say: How do you know when a politician is lying.... because his mouth is moving. This is the definition of politics that causes us to advise City Managers: Be politically aware, but not political. Every elected official should argue for the values and outcomes that they believe in. If that disagreement results in closed mindedness, in disrespecting the will of the majority or using any form of deception, coercion, dishonesty or undermining to get your own way, then it is poor politics.

City Managers should understand that elected officials can, and sometimes will, engage in this form of political behavior, but City Managers need to stay completely out of that fray. Don't allow anyone, no matter how manipulative, subtle or threatening, to draw you into this sort of political gamesmanship. City Managers function inside of a political world but should never get caught up in it. Their job is to lead, advise, manage and engage. It is not to be a politician. Even if no one else in the city has this vision, the City Manager should.

My advice to voters is: Do not reward deceptive, manipulative, undermining, power-hungry politicians by re-electing them. Even if you agree with their stated outcomes, unethical methods will ultimately work to your harm. The ends do not always justify the means. Ethics and integrity are as important in politics as they are in management.

During an election season, one of the candidates was giving out inaccurate information. This surprised me because he had been involved with the city and I thought he knew better. I took occasion to approach him and offer to provide more accurate public information. He told me that he didn't need the information because he already understood the facts. They simply did not fit into his campaign narrative. He was intentionally misleading people; I was shocked. It was an important lesson for me though because it gave me insight to that side of the political system. He won the election and I worked with him for the next four years. But I had to filter and double check everything he said. I also had to be very careful to maintain my ethical standards while tolerating his.

Here is a different example. A Council member used his seat on the City Council as a primary part of his family income, especially the health insurance benefit. I believe he would have done almost anything to retain his seat on the Council. During the election cycle, his strategy was to go door to door and find out what was troubling the person who answered the door. He would then promise to fix the problem if they committed to vote for him. Every few days, I received a list of street conditions people wanted changed, signs that some residents wanted posted, new sidewalks that they wanted installed, etc. It was disingenuous on the part of the Council member, and it short-circuited the budgeting and priority systems that the City Council had in place. The Council member called me at home at all hours of the night and on all days of the week. He was very demanding. When I pushed back by asking him to call me during regular business hours regarding these routine issues, he reminded me that he was my boss and if I didn't give him what he wanted, he would see me fired. I reminded him that I worked for the entire City Council and not for him personally. Still, he vowed to keep his promised threat. It continued to be a strained relationship because he was a politician of the not-so-good sort. After I left the city, he was eventually forced out of office for allegedly fraudulent activity.

So, here's another very important point. No matter how bad the political situation may be, City Managers need to stay out of the election process. I understand that bad conditions may exist and it may appear like the only way to fix things is to get involved in helping good people get elected to the City Council. Even though that may be true, as soon as a City Manager steps over that line, he has violated his own professional standards and surrendered his moral authority. City Managers need to stay out of that part of politics; let the voters deal with those issues. If you can't do that, go find a different job. This is good advice and don't think I didn't learn it through hard experience. There was one time when I actively recruited someone to run for the City Council. He was well qualified and ethical. He won the election and was an asset to the City Council. As hard as I tried to keep my involvement confidential, people found out about it. They always do. The negative effect was that it gave license to some of the Council members to treat me more politically than professionally, which ultimately worked to my detriment. I wished I had never done it, and I never did it again.

Solving Problems

There are two major components of city management that my graduate study did not teach me or was weak on. The first one was how to work with people, the art of City Management. I have previously touched on this issue. The second one is how to solve a problem.

Making decisions and solving problems have a lot in common. The 3-D's (Discover, Debate, Decide) previously discussed in relation to the City Council policymaking are also generally applicable to City Managers as they solve daily problems. Here are the steps to take in solving a problem:

> Define the Problem. Before jumping to a solution, make sure you understand what the problem really is. Don't make assumptions. Dissect it. Define it. Get all the facts. Get clarity about it. A problem well defined is a problem mostly resolved.
> Involve People. Make sure you see the problem from various perspectives. Talk to people. Welcome diverse opinions.

Generate Alternatives. Every issue always has more than one potential solution. Be creative. Keep an open mind. Use group synergy to your advantage.

Calculate Costs. Every solution has a cost. There is also a cost for doing nothing at all and there are lost opportunity costs. It is easy to think short-term but make sure you're also looking long-term. Don't forget about lifecycle costing as well.

Make a Decision. After all the previous work has been done, match the best alternative with the best cost to most effectively address the problem.

Stick to It. Decisions at the City Manager level can always be questioned because there are often other alternative solutions that could have been chosen. If you've done your homework properly, no one will surprise you with an alternative that you have not already thought of; if they do, you are bound to consider it, but you should be a little embarrassed because you were not thorough enough. You should be able to explain why you chose the one you did. There is nothing more disruptive to an organization than wobbly decision-making. Stick to your decision.

Here is an example of a problem that was solved using this process. During the 1970's, when federal money was flowing like water, one3 of my cities received an economic grant to revitalize the historic downtown. They chose to do this by removing the store fronts from several blocks of the downtown area, putting a roof over the street areas and replacing the street system with concrete corridor. This turned the downtown into a shopping mall. The city retained ownership of all the common area where the streets and sidewalks used to be in addition to the HVAC systems. It was also the city's responsibility to provide daily maintenance to those areas. A parking garage was also constructed to serve the mall and the city was responsible for that, as well. Unfortunately, the mall never succeeded as a commercial enterprise because it was more than five miles away from the freeway and traffic flow is vital to the location of any shopping mall. The maintenance costs were excessive. If the city, with its "deep pockets," had not been involved and the private business owners had been required to pay all the operating costs, the mall would have long since failed. By the time I arrived there, the mall was more than 20 years old and the need to replace the HVAC, roofs and parking garage was becoming clear.

After using the problem-solving process outlined above, it became clear that the best alternative solution was to remove the roof and replace the street and store fronts. As costly and painful as that was, it was less costly than continuing with an unsuccessful enterprise. We stuck to the decision and resolved the problem.

Getting the Right Answers

We are all seeking for answers to the questions that trouble us. If you want the right answers, you must first ask the right questions. It takes work and insight to ask the right questions. In fact, this may be the hardest work of all. Insight comes from experience; experience comes from making mistakes; mistakes are painful. Getting the right answers equals wisdom. Wisdom takes time.

Broadcasting City Council Meetings

In one of my cities, the City Council was lobbied by an individual who wanted the city to start an active cable TV station. As part of the franchise agreements that cable TV companies have with cities, the companies must pay a fee for the use of public right-of-way, and they must provide a PEG (Public, Education, Government) channel without cost. This person's proposal was that we activate the channel, purchase the necessary equipment to operate it and hire her to manage it.

I was opposed to the proposal for three reasons. First, I was sincerely afraid that the City Council would play to the cameras, making good decisions even harder to accomplish. Second, the cost of the necessary equipment and the on-going operation costs were significant. It was not budgeted. I thought that the city had higher priorities that were not being met. Third, the idea that someone would lobby the City Council to create a job for herself, skipping all the normal, transparent public process, was repugnant to me. I told the City Council how I felt about it. They politely heard what I had to say, then went on to approve the creation of the TV station and gave me direction to "find the money." I got in line with the City Council's decision and carried out their directive.

I was right: the Council did play to the cameras. Decisions were harder for the City Council. Meetings took longer. I also found that a lot of people watched the meetings and became better informed about city issues. The print media became more accurate and thorough because if they reported something in an inflammatory or inaccurate way, people could watch the actual meeting and decide for themselves what was said or intended. The press could refer to recordings of meetings to make sure their facts and quotations were correct.

Another benefit was increased accountability for both staff and Council. Many times, I have heard City Council members claim that previous staff had not given them all the facts or had given them inaccurate information; if they had known the whole truth, they wouldn't have made such a stupid vote. With a video recording of the meeting, you can know exactly what was presented by the staff; you can see the Council debate and know exactly what they said before they voted. Everyone is held to a more accountable standard.

If a city wanted to get more ambitious, they could use cameras and technology to create information pieces about specific functions and issues within the city and broadcast them as well. We did that in several of the cities I managed.

With the advent of the internet and social media, meetings can be live streamed. Recordings can be archived and accessed by anyone, at any time. Virtual public meetings and hearings can even be held. All of this expands access to city government. It increases knowledge and transparency. I was skeptical at first, but it is all good.

I like to use this as an example of how the wisdom of a multi-body City Council can be greater than that of an individual, even the City Manager.

In Summary, How to Manage City Operations

In this chapter we have considered the third duty of a City Manager, Managing City Operations. To be good at managing a city, one must first clearly understand what cities do and be clear about the city's mission. In general, cities do five things: Public Works, Public Safety, Recreation, Community and Economic Development, and Support Services. Each of these functions have an important part to play in the operations of a city; none are more important than the other. Some may argue that Public Safety, for example, is the most important municipal service. That would certainly be true if you were in the middle of an emergency. But then I would ask what would happen if the emergency vehicle did not have a passable road to respond on? Or what kind of health emergency would be created if the garbage was not collected for a month? What would happen if city personnel were not paid because there was no accounting department? You get my point.

The next thing to understand is the management process itself. In this chapter we have articulated that the process has three primary components: Evaluating, Planning and Execution. Evaluation includes taking stock of current conditions as well as past performance. It eventually means comparing outcomes to previously set internal goals and to external benchmarks. The city's planning process, including budgeting, was outlined in detail. The keys to execution include being crystal clear about expectations and creating a culture of accountability for performance. As any experienced manager will tell you, the process may be simple, but it is not easy.

In addition to the work of the various departments, there are nine systems that function inside of the city and apply to everything that the city does. Those nine systems are: the Governance system, the Management System, the Money system, the People system, the Technology system, the Customer Service system, the Communication system, the Citizen Engagement system, and the Continuous Improvement system. The management process must be applied to these nine systems as well as the service delivery departments.

The chapter is concluded with a series of "Experienced Insights" regarding various topics that every City Manager must deal with. Those topics include budgeting, change management, use of 100-day plans, taking charge of your job, teambuilding, delegation, trust, ensuring that things are happening the way they are reported, the art of city management, hiring people, firing people, unions, keeping emotional distance, total cost decision-making, making presentations, the politics of local government, solving problems, getting the right answers, and broadcasting City Council meetings.

Moving on from here, we'll next cover the fourth duty of a City Manager, engaging people.

ENGAGING
People

Engaging People

The City Manager's Fourth Duty

Attitudes about information are different today than they were when I started my city management career. Expectations are different, too. Over the course of my career, I've had to significantly adjust to be effective in my job. In the old days, cities worked with the local newspaper and relied on them to tell the city's story. The height of informing the citizenry was to send out a printed newsletter with the utility bill. Occasionally an elected official held a neighborhood meeting, but everyone knew that the primary motive behind that was political. Most of the engagement took place at, or related to, the official City Council meeting.

Things are much different today, primarily because of technology. It really wasn't until later in my career that I more fully realized that the world had shifted. It became clear to me that, not only did I need to understand and accept these changes, but I also needed to embrace them.

Before embracing the necessity of engaging, I considered engagement with the community primarily a City Council responsibility. My job was to support them, to carry out the Council's wishes; their job was to connect with their constituents and decide what they wanted out of the city. While that type of thinking is not untrue, it is incomplete. The City Manager's duty is bigger than that. The City Manager has a much bigger role to play in engaging with people. When I arrived at Corpus Christi, I found a newspaper, several TV stations and radio stations all very active in reporting on the city. Feeding off the city would be a more accurate description, and not without good reason. The city was fragmented, disharmonious, and had experienced several ethical breaches that caught the public attention. I needed to change the course of the city and to do that, I needed, among other things, **to engage** the community, the government, the media and the **workforce.**

We live in the information age. **People want** to know what's going on in their city, and they want the **information** on their own terms. This means that they want the information **available,** when they want it, and in the format they prefer. They **also want** to understand what the information means. It is not enough **to simply** know the facts. People today want to understand what is **behind the** facts, the reasons why things are the way they are. Then **they want** to have a say in it. They want to be informed, they want **to be heard and** they want something done. This is the essence of engagement: informing, listening and involving.

Informing

In today's world, cities **can establish** a direct information relationship with their residents **through the** internet, social media and other means. Some of **these communication** tools are two-way, so the city can both **send out** information and receive information back. Cities can, **and should,** tell their own story directly to their constituency. **This does** not preclude or restrict commercial media from telling **the story,** too, but cities are no longer dependent upon them **to accomplish** that task. Cities can, and should, use as much **direct, two-way** communication as possible.

Listening

Listening involves more **than simply** giving polite silence as people pronounce their words. **It means** giving thoughtful attention and consideration to what **they say.** It means seeking to truly understand their point of view. **Every city** has formal mechanisms for listening to people. **These include** public hearings and comment periods during official **meetings** of the city. Listening, communicating and interacting **with people** are art forms. What

I'm talking about in this chapter goes beyond the traditional and formal requirements of city government listening to its people.

Involving

So, what happens after you have informed and listened? For many people, listening to them doesn't do any good, except to cause frustration, if you don't do what they want done. Therein is a great problem. When you're dealing with a population as diverse in opinions as are the American people, getting people to see the broader landscape can be difficult. Helping them to understand and respect the opinions of others can be difficult. One important way to help broaden their horizons is to involve them in the decision-making. This forces them to learn more about issues and receive a breadth of perspective from other people. Again, cities have formal mechanisms to involve people. These include service on boards, commissions, and committees. These are limited to specific numbers of people and generally require a substantial time commitment. Finding ways to involve more people for shorter timeframes is the challenge that City Managers need to address.

Traditionally, many City Managers have left citizen engagement to the elected officials. For a long time, I certainly did, but there is a non-political role that City Managers need to embrace that goes beyond simply supporting elected officials. None of the City Manager's role should diminish or threaten the important role or activities of elected officials. A clear understanding of this duty needs to be had by City Manager and City Council alike. A functional partnership needs to be established that works to the benefit of all the city's residents and the long-term best interest of the city.

Engaging people is a challenging and, for many City Managers, a frightening task. For various reasons, many City Managers shy away from this duty. In today's world, engagement must occur, and the City Manager must ensure that it is happening. The City Manager must engage, and make sure that the city organization is engaging, people. Over the next several sections, I will dissect the duty to Engage by breaking it down into various important groups. In each of those groups, I will, from my experience, explain how to best engage them. Those groups include the following:

1. The Community at large
2. Other Governments
3. The Media
4. The City's Workforce

Engaging the Community

The Community is comprised of residents of all ages and demographics, businesses, non-profit and service organizations, and visitors. It is the most obvious of the four groups to engage and engagement with the Community will help ensure continued trust, confidence and support for the city. It helps connect the city to the people it serves, and it will ensure that the municipal services being delivered are meeting the needs of the people in the best ways possible.

The Community is, of course, comprised of many individuals. Those individuals will disagree with each other on many topics. After receiving a variety of input from community engagement, determining the "voice of the people" can be a very difficult at times. As I have said before, it is the responsibility of the individual City Council members to 1) determine where the majority of opinion lies, 2) compare that with what they believe is the right thing to do, and 3) decide how to vote on any given issue.

City Councils do their work in meetings. The end result of a City Council's work is voting. The purpose and intent of Engagement is to inform and influence the work of the City Council, to inform the outcome of the votes on the City Council so that they can make the most helpful and wise decisions possible. Before the voting takes place, some level of public engagement will always occur. The engagement may be substantial, or it may be minor; it may be formal, or it may be informal. It may be required, or it may be discretionary; it will take place. The intent of this chapter is to better understand community engagement and to discuss ways to help improve both the quality and quantity of civic engagement.

Required Engagement

City Councils are required to establish a regular time and place to hold their meetings. That meeting place and meeting schedule are published and known to the public. The meetings held by City Councils are of various types, as explained below. Each one has a little different level and type of typical engagement. Several Boards and Commissions may also be appointed by the City Council. The purpose of those groups is to either 1) make recommendations to the City Council or 2) take specifically delegated actions on behalf of the City Council. In either case, they are doing part of the work of the City Council and their meetings must be published and open to the public in the same way that the City Council meetings must be. In many cases, Boards and Commissions engage with the public before they make their recommendations to the City Council. Described below is more detail about the required meetings and the community engagement that accompanies those meetings:

> City Council Meetings. In most cities, the law requires that the agendas of all City Council meetings and all committees created under authority of the Council be published in advance of the meetings. This allows people an opportunity to know what the City Council will be discussing and voting on. The intent of that law is, of course, to allow the people time to contact their City Council members or to attend the meeting for the purpose of making their opinions known to their elected officials.

This type of contact is a level of engagement that occurs regularly.

Dependent upon the specific provisions of the City Charter or state law, City Councils generally hold five types of meetings: regular, work sessions, special, emergency and closed.

- Regular Meetings. These are meetings where the routine business of the city is conducted. Agendas are posted in advance of the meeting. The agendas contain the items that the Council will be discussing and voting on. The Council may not discuss or vote on any item that has not been properly posted on an agenda. This ensures that the community is informed and has an opportunity to engage their elected officials. During the meeting, items are presented to the City Council by the staff and the City Council votes to approve or disapprove the items. Some City Charters require that each item receive two separate readings before the vote. This means that an item is presented at one meeting but not voted on until a subsequent meeting. Again, this allows time for more community engagement.

  Engagement for regular meetings generally consists of informal input where community members contact their elected officials by phone, email, text or letter in advance of the meeting to discuss an item and make their thoughts on it known. There is also a degree of formal engagement if the community member attends the meeting and publicly speaks to the issue before the vote. In most instances, the engagement is initiated by the community member.

- Work Sessions. These are learning sessions for the City Council. Council members receive briefings and reports, get introduced to future agenda items and ask relevant questions. The topics for discussion are posted on an official agenda in the same way as regular meetings. Except for giving non-binding direction to the City Manager, the City Council does not vote on items during their work sessions. All items that require action from the City Council will move from a work session to the regular meeting agenda for a vote.

Typically, there is no formal engagement at Work Sessions, and community members are not allowed to speak to the issues being discussed. The intent of Work Sessions is for the City Council to become familiar with issues and get their questions answered. Engagement for work session meetings consists of informal input, where a community member first learns about the item, then contacts their elected officials by phone, email, text or letter to discuss an item and make their thoughts on it known. Generally, this happens after the Work Session because, before then, neither the Council nor the community members have a full working understanding of the issue. In most instances, the engagement is initiated by the community member. Occasionally a City Council member will seek input from select constituents between work sessions and regular meetings.

- Special Meetings. These are typically meetings of the City Council which are outside of the normal meeting schedule and have a single topic of special interest. If a vote on the special meeting topic is anticipated, it must be legally advertised on the agenda. There will be specific provisions and requirements for special meetings outlined in the City Charter or the state law. Generally, the terms and conditions of a special meeting will be clarified and articulated on the published agenda. If a vote is anticipated, the meeting will be handled like a regular meeting.

Engagement for a special meeting will vary, depending on the terms and conditions set in advance by the City Council. Engagement may resemble either that of the regular or work session or a hybrid of both.

- Emergency Meetings. On rare occasion, something will happen that requires City Council action before the next regular meeting. Under those emergent conditions, the law allows for emergency meetings. Notice of the meeting must be given and agendas must still be posted, but the time frames for notice are shorter. Typically, instead of a 72-hour posting requirement, it may only be 24 hours. In some cases, only notice to the press is required. There will be specific provisions and requirements for emergency meetings outlined in the City Charter or the state law.

  Two of the cities I worked in had a Charter requirement for two readings on agenda items before the City Council could vote on them unless the item was declared an emergency. If it was declared an emergency, it could be voted on with only one reading. When I arrived in both of those cities, it was standard practice to declare every item an emergency so that the business of the city could be acted upon in one meeting and move more quickly. In the first city, it took me several years to realize that the authors of the Charter knew what they were talking about. Following that understanding, I recommended following the Charter by having two separate readings. Emergency declarations should not be used for routine business; they should be used for true emergent conditions. There is wisdom in allowing time for Community Engagement to take place. It only took me a few weeks in the second city to make the same recommendation.

  Engagement for an emergency meeting will be the same as for a regular meeting.

- <u>Closed (Executive Session) Meetings.</u> The law allows for certain limited exceptions to the open public meetings laws. When the exceptions are met, the City Council meeting may be closed to the public. Qualifying exceptions include discussing legal strategy when the city is being, or may be, sued; real estate transactions strategy where public disclosure of the transaction would be harmful to the city; union contract negotiating strategy and certain Personnel actions that could be legally harmful to the city or to the person being discussed. The scope of these Executive Sessions is very limited. The fact that the City Council will hold a closed meeting must be posted on an agenda, along with the general qualifying topic. After closed discussion, any resulting decision and vote must be executed in public.

  Of necessity, Community Engagement on closed meetings is very limited, generally because the public does not know the details of the issue until well after it is resolved.

- <u>Public Hearings.</u> Public Hearings are formal proceedings designed to allow all interested parties to speak to an issue. Depending on the state in which a city is located, Public Hearings are required prior to certain decisions of the City Council being made. Examples include zoning changes, annexations, budget adoption and increases in the property tax rate. Agendas for Public Hearings, along with the time and place of the hearing, are published in advance and the City Council is obligated to receive public input prior to voting. City Councils may impose rules for comments received at Public Hearings, such as time limits or the necessity to address all comments to the Chair of the meeting. Public Hearings are generally a separate part of the City Council's regular meeting, and they may also be part of a special meeting. Although community members may approach the City Council members informally prior to the meeting, the Public Hearing is intended specifically to formally hear from members of the community. It is a formal and substantial form of Community Engagement.

Boards, Commissions and Committees. Every City Council will appoint members of the community to serve on various Boards, Commissions and Committees. Each of the groups is given specific tasks and scopes of work, in most cases to make recommendations for City Council action. Some groups may be delegated limited decision-making responsibility of their own. Some Boards and Commissions are required under State law or City Charter; some are created at the discretion of the City Council. Even though not all Boards and Commissions are required by law, I am covering them all in this section because they are all intended to engage citizens in the decision-making requirements of the city and to receive public input for the City Council prior to making those decisions. Examples of the groups include: The Planning and Zoning Commission, the Board of Building Appeals, the Park Board, the Animal Control Advisory Committee, the Senior Citizen's Board, etc. There are many Boards and Commission that function in a city with potentially hundreds of people being involved.

City Managers should be constantly aware that appointments to Boards and Commissions is a political process and, as such, it belongs entirely to the elected policy makers. The Council' appointment process may be frustrating at times and it may cause more work for staff, but City Managers should keep their noses out of the it.

I recall an instance that provides a good example. I was receiving a performance evaluation from the City Council one year. It was a good review and I shared a good mutual working relationship with the City Council.

However, some of the City Council were beginning to get more involved in the administration of the city than the Charter or good practice allowed. I mentioned it to the Council and they all immediately agreed to fix the encroachment. When my evaluation was concluded, they began to address another matter of Personnel, the appointment of people to serve on the Planning Commission. I understood the appointment to be a political one but, in this instance, I had a strong feeling about it. So, I made my thoughts known to the City Council. I was immediately reminded by one of the Council members that it was right for the Council to stay out of my business, as they had just agreed, and it was right for me to stay out of their business. He was right. I said no more. Lesson learned.

There may be rare instances when the city code requires the City Manager to make certain appointments to a board. For example, in one of my cities, it was the City Manager's responsibility, under city ordinance, to appoint members to the Civil Service Commission. In another city, it was the City Manager's responsibility to appoint members to the Animal Services Advisory Committee which was a highly controversial and very political appointment. My experience tells me that, except for limited scope ad hoc committees designed to give advice only to the City Manager, appointments to city Boards, Commissions and Committees should be made by the City Council. If there are instances where City ordinance requires the City Manager to make appointments, they should be closely examined with an eye toward shifting the appointment responsibility back to the City Council. Appointment to Boards, Commissions and Committees is a political process. This is true even for the Civil Service Commission where their work involves ensuring that employees are being treated fairly (a City Manager responsibility), and that Civil Service rules are being followed. Perhaps in the instance of Civil Service, a degree of independence from the City Manager is even more required to ensure good and fair treatment of the workforce since it would be the City Manager's administration allegedly violating good employment practice.

Engagement for Boards, Commissions and Committees occurs in three ways. First, the appointment to the group in the first place is an act of engagement initiated by the City Council. Second, the appointees make recommendations to the City Council. Third, in many cases the groups reach out to even more community members to get input before they make recommendations to the City Council.

Discretionary Engagement

In addition to the required engagement described above, there are several other things that can be done to engage people. These things are not required; they are discretionary. These discretionary engagements may be as important to meet the expectations of the community as the required ones. Discretionary engagement includes things like the following examples:

City Council Sponsored Community Engagement Meetings. Often, elected officials will hold meetings to connect with and inform their constituency. Because many operational questions are asked at these meetings and because such meetings require logistical support, the City Manager will most likely be called upon to support, or assign staff to support, these efforts. Because they can be energy and resource intensive, the City Council needs to establish policy outlining the parameters within which these types of meetings may be held. The meetings are important to help keep constituencies informed; caution needs to be exercised when meetings are scheduled near election times. City Councils have a duty to lead and inform their constituencies but may not use city resources to promote their personal political campaigns. Because it is unethical and, in most cities, illegal, no one wants to give the impression that public resources are being used to support the individual campaign efforts of incumbent members of the City Council. The types of City Council sponsored meetings may include the following:

- District Informational Meetings. It is common for cities to divide themselves into equally populated City Council Districts where each District elects a representative to sit on the City Council. The intent is to ensure that all geographic and social areas of the city have representation. In some cases, the courts have mandated such arrangements to ensure social justice. In those cases, half or more of the City Council will be elected from geographic districts. Elected officials who represent districts will sometimes hold informational meetings for members of their district. Topics of discussion typically include current items the City Council is dealing with, updates on capital projects and updates on other items of interest to the group.

  Engagement at District Meetings is less formal than at regular City Council meetings and there is generally much more give and take between the parties in attendance. At these meetings, City Council members have an excellent opportunity to inform and lead their constituencies. They also have an excellent opportunity to listen and hear their constituencies.

- Town Hall Meetings. These meetings are similar in purpose and function to District Meetings except that they are more general. People from any part of the city may attend and the At-Large members of the City Council are also participants in the meeting. Topics of discussion for these meetings are like the District Meetings described above.

  Engagement at Town Hall Meetings is less formal than at regular City Council meetings, and there is generally much more give and take between the parties in attendance. At these meetings, City Council members have an excellent opportunity to inform and lead their constituencies. They also have an excellent opportunity to listen to and hear their constituencies. Because Town Hall Meetings are generally bigger, certainly more elected officials are in attendance and more structure and control are required than District Meetings.

- Individual Constituent Meetings. Council Members will meet from time to time with constituents who have specific questions or opinions they wish to share. Oftentimes, their questions have to do with city operations rather than policy. Operations, of course, are the purview of the City Manager. As such, the City Manager or an assigned staff member will generally need to assist the elected official in answering operational questions. Things certainly work better if the elected official invites the help, and the City Manager is willing to give it. Too often, City Council members are unwilling or embarrassed to admit that they are not responsible for day-to-day operations. Too often constituents will inappropriately demand that their elected official deal with an operational issue. When that happens and the City Manager is not involved in resolving operational issues, things just get tangled up.

Staff-Sponsored Community Engagement Meetings. These are meetings initiated by the City Manager. The purposes of the meeting are to 1) inform people about the operational activities of the city and current topics of interest, 2) hear concerns about operational issues, 3) instruct people in how the city government works, 4) allow people to interact personally with the appointed leadership of the city and 5) take work orders for services or problems that need to be resolved.

It should be made very clear that these meetings are not the same as those initiated by the City Council; these are focused entirely on city operations, not policy. Their purpose is to address the issues that are difficult or impossible for elected officials to appropriately cover during their meetings although some City Council members may wish to attend these meetings and should be welcome to do so.

For purposes of explanation, I will divide staff-sponsored Engagement meetings into two categories:

- Departments. Departments provide services to the city. Of necessity they must interact with and engage their customers. This is true of all departments and the best example I can think of is the Police Department. Police departments are generally active in crime prevention. Part of that effort includes having people assigned to Neighborhood Crime Watch which holds regular meetings with citizens. Sometimes the crime watch effort expands into a full-blown community relations program. In many cities, in addition to neighborhood watch meetings, the Police Department might hold regular community meetings to report on crime trends and special enforcement efforts and to engage residents in helping to make the city a safer place to live. As I said, other Departments do similar things in alignment with their missions though generally not as extensively as the Police Department.

- <u>City Manager.</u> In a couple of my cities, I elevated the concept of Department Meetings to a city-wide effort by holding community meetings at various locations throughout the city, generally two or three times per year. The format for the meeting included having tables where various Department heads were seated, and citizens could visit the table and talk directly to the Department Head. Questions were answered and issues discussed directly with the person responsible for providing the service. We had city employees in attendance to make work orders when the discussion resulted in a commitment to act on a service request. Also included was a 15-minute presentation by the City Manager with questions and answers relating to a current topic, such as the budget, current capital projects or a difficult issue recently resolved. No operational question was off limits. Current policy questions could be trickier to answer without preempting or disrupting the City Council's policy-making process. If policy questions were asked regarding issues currently under debate, I would evade the question, outline the policy-making process and invite them to learn more by watching City Council meetings or by engaging with their elected officials.

In the last of these meetings I held, Texas, we began experimenting with streaming the meeting over social media. I believe there is a great opportunity to expand community Engagement using electronic and social media.

Engaging Other Governments

Cities are part of a federal system of government, meaning that they are among other layers of government such as the National, State, and other local governments. The US constitution recognizes two levels of government, the National and State governments. Local governments, including cities, are created under authority of the States. That is why they are sometimes referred to as "creatures of the State." It is important that cities work with all other governments in the Federal system. It is very important for cities to have a voice with the National and State government because those governments have power to legislate burdensome and costly requirements on Cities. Local governments don't have the same authority as the National and State governments; building coalitions and partnerships with other local governments is important to 1) help influence the State legislature and National congress, 2) to cooperate on issues of local concern where jurisdictional interests cross or compete and, 3) to handle emergencies and disasters with the most efficiency possible. The value of creating strong partnerships at all these levels cannot be over emphasized. Here are some observations about engaging with other governments:

The National Government

The Congress, the Supreme Court and various Federal Agencies all have an impact on city government. Laws are passed by Congress; the constitutionality of those laws is judged by the Supreme Court; the Federal Agencies make the rules to apply the laws; then they administer and enforce them. Sometimes it seems that everything a city does is impacted by the National Government. Examples include mirandizing someone who has been arrested, maintaining water quality standards, hiring practices, working hours and labor practices, access for the handicapped, radio communication frequencies, operation of airports, highway construction standards, public transit systems and provision of programs for moderate- and low-income persons. The list is endless.

Getting to know your Member of Congress and your Senators is very important. Often, getting to know their staff members is even more practical for getting routine things done. Some larger cities hire lobbyists located in the nation's capital so that they can stay abreast of issues and represent a city's interest on a continuing basis. Many cities are members of the National League of Cities, one of whose primary purposes is to be aware of developing policies of the National Government. They have an annual conference in Washington DC where local officials are not only schooled in their responsibilities but encouraged to visit with Members of Congress in their offices to maintain good working relations.

The impact of Federal Agencies should not be underestimated. Acronyms like EPA, DOJ, FHA, DHHS, USDOT, GSA, SSA, FBI, OSHA, DEA, Census Bureau, Corps of Engineers, DOL, ATFE, etc., are well known to many cities. Knowing who to talk to and maintaining relationships directly, or through agents, with these agencies can be very helpful when issues arise.

The issue of "unfunded mandates" for cities has become increasingly sensitive and important over the years. An unfunded mandate is a law or rule created by a higher level of government which Cities are required to follow. Compliance with those laws and rules is costly, but no offsetting revenue source is given by the mandating government. Cities have no choice but to comply and pass the accompanying costs on to their residents. I am unaware of any authoritative study regarding the cost of unfunded mandates on city governments, but my best guess is that half, or more, of a city budget is required because of unfunded mandates from either the State or National governments. Then, when State legislatures place limitations on local taxation, as they often do, it puts cities in an even tighter bind. They require the spending on the one hand and limit the city's ability to pay for it on the other hand. When unfunded mandates occur in this manner, they appear to be both politically motivated and disingenuous.

Again, I should be clear. I'm not saying that a specific subject of a mandate, like clean water or clean air, etc., is unnecessary or negative policy. I'm just saying that everyone should honestly realize that it places a significant financial burden on city government. Along with the mandate, cities should be given leeway, authority and assistance in managing those financial burdens.

The City Manager needs to be current on things that are happening in Washington to effectively advise the City Council. Strong relations need to be maintained in the good times so that, during the difficult times, problems can be resolved. The City Manager must ensure that the city is engaged with the National government.

In one of my cities and prior to my arrival, there had been an effort to widen a nearby river and make it a more useful amenity. This was proposed to be done by dredging out a substantial portion of the river, giving it more of the appearance of a lake. Because the river was considered part of the waters of the United States, excavation approval was required from the US Corps of Engineers. The process was lengthy and slow so the work started without formal approval from the appropriate government agency. Nothing but trouble followed. There were lawsuits and threats to withhold federal funding on other projects, including the city's airport, block grants, transit system and proposed road projects. It took many meetings, a lot of negotiation, a lot of relationship building and a consent decree (legal settlement) to bring that conflict to resolution. This would be a good case study in what happens when a city fails to engage its federal government partners.

The State Government

The ties between cities and the State government are very strong. Absent the State government, cities would not exist; cities are "creatures" of the State, as explained earlier in this book. Cities function by either Dillon's Rule, which states that cities have only those rights expressly given to them by the State, or by Charter, again, allowed by the State but defined locally about what the authority, process, duties, and limitations for governing the city will be.

As with the National Government, it is good for a city to know their State Representatives and Senators and to develop good working relations with them. It is common for State elected officials to not understand how Cities operate or what issues challenge them. A little information and understanding goes a long way; cities are well benefitted by staying in touch with their state decision-makers. It is a lot easier to prevent a bad piece of legislation than it is to fix it after the fact. For this reason, most cities are members of a state-wide League of Cities whose purpose is to ensure that State government understands the challenges facing cities and the impacts of proposed legislation on their member cities. Additionally, some cities hire lobby firms to represent their interests. Larger cities typically have full-time intergovernmental relations staff to help maintain relationships and coordinate the work of lobbyists.

Because the primary purpose of cities is to provide every day, basic service to people and not to create controversial social or tax policy, most City Council Members are elected on a non-partisan basis. That is not true of State-elected officials. While everyone knows that nearly every City Council Member is affiliated with a political party, that partisan gap between city and State officials needs to be bridged without compromising the intent of non-partisan elected positions in cities.

The operation of State Legislatures varies widely. For example, some states have full-time legislatures that are constantly in session. Other states have part-time legislatures that meet only every other year for a limited amount of time. Many have repeated the quotation attributed to both Mark Twain and Gideon Tucker, "No man's life, liberty, or property are safe while the legislature is in session." I have found this sentiment to be particularly true for the impact of legislatures on cities. Staying vigilant regarding the State government is a good thing for cities.

Legislatures can appear to be very slow moving and boring as they organize themselves at the beginning of a session. A lot of the positioning is done behind closed doors in party "caucuses." Then they can move very quickly as items progress through committee and onto the floor for voting. Someone from the city needs to be present during all of this and prepared to testify before committee and to meet with elected representatives at a moment's notice to explain details and impacts of proposed legislation on the city they represent. The better this part of the work is done by cities the more unintended consequences will be avoided on the back end of the process.

While I was in Texas, I found it useful for the cities I worked in to adopt legislative goals or principles for upcoming legislative sessions so that staff and lobbyists can follow those goals as they react to the quick moving decisions of the legislature. The Council position should include both offensive (things to be achieved) and defensive (things to be prevented) goals formally adopted by the Council. This is because individual Council Members may disagree on some points and those speaking on behalf of the city must know that they have the authority and backing of the City Council, as expressed by an approved resolution.

All the above comments deal with the making of law. Once the law has been enacted, there is a requirement to administer and enforce it. So, not only is it important that a city have a relationship with the law-making part of State government, but also with the state bureaucracy.

Similarly, as with the National government, the City Manager needs to be aware of what's happening at the State House. Otherwise, effectively advising the City Council can be difficult. Strong relations need to be maintained in the good times so that problems can be avoided or resolved later. The City Manager must ensure that the city is engaged with the State government.

Corpus Christi, Texas, has a substantial oil refining industry. Much of the oil comes into the refineries through a ship channel which connects them to the Gulf of Mexico. There is a bridge over the ship channel allowing ground traffic to move along the coast. While I was in Corpus Christi, Texas, it became apparent that the bridge needed to be replaced. This was a $1 billion project, clearly too big for any one entity to accomplish. For years, strong partnerships had been formed between the TxDOT, Federal Highway Administration, the State Legislature, the counties and surrounding cities, the Port of Corpus Christi, various neighborhood groups, the business community and the City of Corpus Christi. This project required the engaged partnership of many groups and is a good example of how good partnerships work to the benefit of all concerned.

I recall another, not so good, example from my experience in another state. My city, along with all other cities in the state, belonged to a State Retirement System. It was a defined benefit system, meaning that the end retirement benefit for individuals was determined by the number of years in the system, multiplied by the average of one's highest three years of compensation, multiplied by some fixed percentage. It was not determined by how much money had been contributed to the account; that would be a defined contribution system. Periodically, the Retirement System would tell the cities what percentage of their total payroll needed to be contributed to the Retirement System. The required contribution had become unreasonably burdensome. As I recall now, it was more than 20%. Although we, and I personally, had testified before the legislative oversight committee, the Retirement System was immovable and unsympathetic to the burdensome and ever-increasing costs. After some time of trying to resolve this issue, a recommendation was made to the City Council that the city withdraw from the State Retirement System and form its own retirement plan. They agreed. A great defined contribution plan was formed, which finally capped the retirement costs to the city. Because I was new to the city management profession, I did not realize there would be unanticipated consequences. Other cities throughout the state followed our example and withdrew from the State System, enough so that it changed the actuarial projections and threatened the viability of the State System. Within a few years, the legislature was forced to act by retroactively passing new legislation requiring all cities to re-enter and participate in the State System. New provisions allowed ten percent of the city's workforce to be exempt from state participation, but everyone else was compelled. Looking back, I wish we would have made a bigger effort to build partnerships and more substantially engage with the legislature, the State Retirement System and colleague cities to resolve that problem. Good things finally happened, but it was a very long way around it, and relationships were damaged in the process.

Counties

Like cities, Counties are political subdivisions of the state. They generally differ from cities in that they 1) serve the population residing outside of an incorporated city by providing a limited number of municipal-type services such as, roads, drainage, planning and zoning, law enforcement, and, 2) serve all residents of the County, including those who reside inside of a city, by administering social services programs; providing courts that deal with felonies and higher level issues, whereas city courts are restricted to misdemeanors; providing property records and tax administration; providing legal services to support the courts; providing health department services; providing coroner services; sometimes providing parks and recreation services; and providing jails.

Care needs to be taken so that municipal residents are not double taxed, which can easily happen if taxes from cities are used to underwrite the municipal-type services provided to unincorporated parts of the County. Conflict often arises over annexation issues where cities desire to increase their jurisdictional boundaries. These potential conflicts only increase as our country grows in population and we become more urbanized.

To minimize potential conflicts, City Managers need to clearly understand the service differences between cities and counties and to remain engaged with the county government. Knowing the county officials and interacting with them regularly helps a great deal.

One of my cities went through a period of annexation to expand its borders for economic development purposes. Even though individual property owners were favorable, the county into which the city expanded was opposed to the annexation, as were the township officials. The opposition was predictable because the political entities had conflicting and competing interests. The City Council, however, determined that it was in the best interest of the city to proceed. I became City Manager after that had occurred. I vividly recall the animosity that existed toward the city. It took years of ethical, candid relationship building to begin to overcome some of that animosity. Some of it never went away. It wasn't just animosity. There was undermining at the legislature on key issues and on mutual interest projects that came along later. I can't help but believe that higher levels of engagement, dialog, patience and perhaps a little compromise would have netted better results for everyone.

Other Cities

Cities are sometimes in competition with each other, for example, when a company is trying to decide where to locate their operation or if two adjacent communities are trying to enlarge their borders into the same area. For the most part, cities are much better off when they cooperate, rather than when they compete. Examples of cooperation include public safety mutual aid agreements, regionally owned and operated water plants, and other types of shared service agreements.

The same rules of candor, honesty and integrity should apply between cities as between individuals. Entities don't interact with each other, individual people do. Trust is built because of the ethical conduct of the parties involved.

It has been my experience that professional administrators can get along and communicate well even when elected officials cannot. It is good for neighboring City Managers to meet periodically, just to get to know each other or to discuss issues of common interest. This relationship becomes very valuable when contentious issues come up. Whatever way it is done, City Managers need to ensure that they are engaged with both neighboring and other cities throughout the state. To this end, it is helpful for City Managers to belong to the statewide association of City Managers that exists in virtually every state.

In another of my cities, there was rapid growth and expansion. There was conflict with surrounding communities because of the annexation practices and requirements, particularly on our southern border. Anticipating the problems and trying to avoid as much unnecessary conflict as possible, the City Administrator of that city and I met on multiple occasions to try to work things out.

The result of our work was a border agreement for future growth that we both took back to our respective City Councils. The agreement was approved by both cities and it avoided a lot of potential conflict. This was a good example of how engagement paid off.

School Districts

It is easy for cities to misjudge the importance of their relationship to the school districts that serve their common citizenry. Although the missions of the School District and the city are completely different, they are very much in competition for the tax base. Cities generally have access to sales tax that School Districts don't; Schools have access to State allotments that Cities don't. Both cities and School Districts are heavily dependent upon property tax to support their operations and that is where potential competition arises. If you were to examine the itemized property tax bill in a county, in almost every case, it would show the School District getting the lion's share of the total property tax revenue. It is not uncommon for both cities and School Districts to have bond issues on the ballot at the same time. As a practical matter, those elections should be coordinated between the two entities so that success for both can be more often realized.

School Districts serve the children and families of the community. So does the city. Cities also serve the School Districts. When a school is placed in a community, it requires road access and maintenance, sidewalks, school crossings, crossing guards, school zone lights and enforcement, city utilities and police and fire support. The duty to serve schools does not mean that cities should become slaves to the school system. This can happen when there is not a proper amount of communication between the two entities and decisions are being made that affect the other without that communication having taken place. This is particularly true about future planning for and placement of new schools. School Districts can, de facto, impose substantial expenses on cities with their placement of new schools. Schools pass bond levies for the construction of those new schools but the cost of roads, utility expansion, sidewalks, traffic control devices, etc. are not included in those bonds. Those costs fall to the city. The more communication and the stronger the partnerships are between city and school, the more those types of problems could be avoided. I have faced this type of problem in every city I have managed. It would be ideal to have companion bond issues on the same ballot to support all the costs of constructing a new school, those borne by the School District and those borne by the city.

The City Manager needs to be current with respect to things that are happening in the School District to effectively advise the City Council. Strong relations need to be maintained so that conflicts can be avoided. The City Manager must ensure that the city is engaged with the School Districts that operate inside of its jurisdiction.

Special Service Districts

In many states, cities have authority to create special service districts to provide elevated levels of service to a specific portion of the community for an additional fee. I'm not talking here about that type of Special Service District because, in that type of district, the city remains in charge of both operations and revenue; no additional engagement is necessary. I'm talking about regional Special Service Districts of which the city is only a fractional part. Examples include Water Districts, Sewer Districts, Law Enforcement Districts, Fire Service Districts, Regional Dispatching Service Districts, Regional Parks Districts, etc. In this regional type of District, the city typically has a representative that sits on a governing or coordinating Board. So, the city has influence but not control. The effectiveness of that Board participation usually goes beyond a single personality sitting on a Board. In these ventures, it is particularly important that the City Manager, City Council and other officials maintain good working relations and stay engaged with the partners so that the best interests of the city can be achieved through regional partnerships.

Councils of Governments

Councils of Government (COG) are voluntary organizations (although some states have mandated them) which are comprised of the counties and cities within their boundaries. They are generally controlled by their member entities and they may deal with regional planning, community and economic development, transit planning, transportation coordination, human services delivery, water use, emergency planning and coordination, analysis of demographic and geographic data, public safety issues and any other issue of regional concern that the member entities agree to tackle.

Metropolitan Planning Organizations (MPO) can be separate from the COG and they focus their mission on transportation, specifically the coordination and administration of Federal Highway monies. All the MPO's I have dealt with are part of the COG. These are organizations that coordinate and prioritize regional issues of concern between local governments.

The topics COGs and MPOs deal with are integral to a city's mission. It is of vital importance that the city be represented in these organizations and that the city be engaged by participating in their activities.

Engaging the Media

When I say "Media", I mean newspaper, radio, TV, internet website and social media of all sorts. Early in my career, it was common for City Managers to avoid the media as something that could hurt both them and the cities they served. And, indeed, there was a degree of truth in those fears because 1) cities had little or no direct mass access to their people and 2) intense competition among and between media outlets would cause them to bend the truth or sensationalize portions of it to suit their own needs. The common use of technology has since changed all of that.

One of the unanticipated benefits of videotaping and broadcasting City Council meetings was that the newspaper reporting regarding the city improved noticeably after the broadcasts began. The accuracy and impartiality improved because a lot more people had direct access to seeing the actual meeting and not just reading a reporter's or editor's interpretation of the meeting. The reporters wanted to get their facts straight so that criticisms would be invalidated.

The Media should not be feared or avoided. The Media is a valuable resource to be engaged with skill and confidence in the furtherance of the city's mission. City Managers need to engage with the media.

Not all cities have access to all the various media types but all cities have access to at least some of them. Certainly, all cities can have access to the internet and social media.

My observations about engaging the media are as follows:

General Observations

Regarding outside commercial media sources, their practice is not just to inform but rather to persuade. The Media decision-makers exercise personal political agendas as they select the stories and as they consider newsworthy events to report. When I first started my career, opinions were limited to the editorial page or editorial comment on the TV. Today, opinion is blended with the facts of the story so that it takes a very astute reader, listener or viewer to discern the difference. This is true on the national level as well as the local level. Headlines and TV teasers can be misleading to grab attention. These issues lead to a natural hesitancy on the part of some City Managers to engage with the media. Even with these problems, it is a mistake to shut the media out. The City Manager must engage them with personal and professional integrity despite media's potential disregard for their own journalistic integrity. Don't assist them in journalistic deception; give them the truth and use all the media resources available, including direct ones under the control of the city to make sure the facts are fully disclosed and the truth is told even if it may be painful to tell it. Trust the people to discern truth from error.

Things That Make News

There are certain things that make news. They just do. Get prepared for them; use them to your advantage if you can. Avoid problems when you can. Certainly, get out in front of the issue when you can. Those things include this:

Sex. Anything related to sexual abuse or misconduct will draw media attention. Issues of this nature are best prevented rather than explained after the fact.

Children. If it relates to children, opportunities for them or abuses of them, it will draw media attention.

Minorities. Especially unfair treatment or perceived unfair treatment will get the attention of media.

Taxes, Fees and Budgets. If you mess with someone's pocketbook, get ready for a media story.

Controversy among Elected Officials. As a City Manager you may have influence with your bosses, but you will certainly not control them. If they get nasty with each other, or even if they simply disagree, it will be newsworthy.

Anything That Can Be Made to Look Like a Controversy. It doesn't even need to be true. Simple disagreements, especially between average citizens and City Hall or between elected officials, can be made to appear more controversial than they really are. Get ready to deal with it.

Animals. Today, people love their pets more than they like some other human beings. If there is a hint of animal mistreatment, be prepared to deal with it.

Scandal. Any type of scandal at City Hall will be newsworthy. In fact, it doesn't even need to be true. It just needs to be a rumor. After Watergate, every reporter fancies herself as an investigative reporter. Again, this type of issue is better prevented through ethical behavior than explained.

Crime. Most media have a reporter assigned to the police department crime blotter. Most Police Departments have media specialists on their staff to accommodate reporters. Policies should be in place to notify City Managers of crimes that get high levels of public attention because commenting on them is not limited to the Police Department and the reporters will request it without warning.

Knowing that at least the above topics will be newsworthy, preparing in advance to deal with them is much better than reacting after the fact. There is an old adage that holds true: When you're explaining, you're losing. Always prepare for and get out in front of the story.

Tips for Dealing with Reporters

If you've never engaged much with the media, the following tips may be useful:

Know your subject and facts. Even though many reporters are well researched and prepared, you are the subject matter expert. Think and prepare before you speak. You must master the subject and know your facts. Most of the time, that means that you need to know the topic of the interview prior to accepting the interview. This will allow you time to prepare. You may meet with resistance from some media reporters regarding this because they want a shocked spontaneous reaction; it makes you look guilty and, therefore, controversial. That type of reaction helps their ratings. You need to know what you're talking about and you need to be prepared. Do what you must to ensure that happens.

Never lie, ever. Don't hire someone else to lie for you, either. If you're a City Manager and you have a problem telling the truth, you should seriously consider a different line of work. Reporters are a naturally suspicious group of people. They look for the lie and they're good at finding it. If they think you are dishonest with them, they will be relentless and give you no peace. They will test you. Never give them cause to doubt your candor. If you lie, they will justifiably shred you like an old garment. If there is something you can't talk about due to timing or legally required confidentiality, tell them you can't talk about it now, but you will when you can. Avoid saying "No comment" because it makes you look guilty of something. Guilty equals controversy. Controversy equals its own news, even if it's not true.

Know what you want to say. Before an interview, understand clearly what two or three points you want to make. A reporter can and will ask whatever questions they want. Keep this in mind: them asking, doesn't mean you're obligated to answer. Sometimes reporters, especially new ones to the industry, don't even know what questions they should ask; you may need to help them ask the right questions. The points you want to make may or may not relate to the questions the reporter asks. Before the interview is over, make sure you deliver your message, as well as trying to be responsive to the reporter's questions.

Learn To Bridge. A bridge gets you from one topic to a different topic. A reporter may ask an irrelevant question or one you can't answer at that time, or you may need to make one of your three important points. Use a bridge to get to a different topic. Some bridge phrases include:

- The better question is….
- The real point is….
- Some people think that….
- You can also look at it this way….
- The more important topic is ….
- Let me be clear about….

Respect Deadlines. Every reporter is on a deadline to get to print or air. Respecting and helping them meet their deadlines will help build the relationship. Besides, it's just plain professional courtesy.

Never speak "Off the Record". First, you should always consider yourself "On the Record" because you are. Saying, "Off the record," before making a comment doesn't mean that you won't be quoted. If you don't want to read it, hear it, or see it on commercial media, don't say it.

Embargo. This is a press release put out in advance of an event with a stipulation for a date and time that it can become public information. It is part of journalistic ethics to respect embargos; all professional media outlets and reporters do.

Background. Occasionally a complicated topic will come up where it would be helpful to everyone for reporters to thoroughly understand the topic rather than just picking up fragmented comments from public dialog. If they agree to not release the information prior to a specified time, reporters can be briefed in advance. This is called "Background." Any comments you make during the background briefing are fair game for quoting in a story. They simply will not report the story until after the subject is made public by the city. Ethical reporters will honor an agreed upon Background briefing. However, some of them may use the information they received in the Background to get quotations from other sources. By doing so, they have not technically violated their Background agreement. Therefore, a background briefing should be as close to the actual public release of the information as possible. Be cautious.

Good News. For the most part, good news doesn't play with commercial media. They like controversy and sensationalism much better. It will be a rare occasion that the media covers a good news story. You can try but you will probably need to find another outlet for getting good news to your public audience.

Newspapers

This is the most common and the most commonly available of all the commercial media for most cities. There was a time in my career when the newspaper was the only effective way to communicate with city residents. That is not true anymore because of the availability of the other media. In fact, financial competition between media sources has created a unique condition in dealing with newspapers. Most newspapers are struggling to remain in business which means, from my observation, that they have sometimes reverted to sensationalism in their reporting so that they can maintain market share and be more competitive. At the end of the day, none of this changes the professionalism with which City Managers should treat them.

Get To Know the Reporter. It helps to know the reporter assigned to the city beat. Keep in mind that the reporters don't get to write the headline; even the content of the article can be rewritten by an editor. Having a reporter who desires to understand an issue before writing about it and gets their facts straight, is a tremendous benefit to the city.

Knowing the reporter helps with all of that. At the same time, don't expect to be friends with a reporter; don't even try. Good reporters won't let that happen. The best you should hope for is that the reporter will get the facts straight and tell both sides of a controversial story with accuracy.

Meet with the Editorial Board. Newspapers always have an editorial page. The content of that page is governed by the Editorial Board. That board is generally made up of the Publisher, the Editor, other newspaper staff, and a couple of community members. They will almost always publish opinion about local affairs in the city. I have found it very helpful to meet with them personally, candidly answer their questions, and make sure they understand the city's and City Manager's position on issues. This relationship matters.

My experience in two cities had many differences, including my attitude. I had been invited many times to appear before the editorial board of the local newspaper in City #1. I regularly declined the invitation, thinking the newspaper to be adversarial and biased against the city. In City #2, I initiated meetings with the editorial board even though they had been critical of the city because I wanted the city's story told. I welcomed their insightful and challenging questions. I wanted them to know what my plan for the city was, write what they may about it. Certainly, they maintained their independence, and I think the engagement helped. I wish I had done more of it in City #1.

Manage Your Own Expectations. Sometimes new City Managers have unrealistic expectations about their relationship with the newspaper. These are examples:

- What they write about. Don't ever think you can or should tell a reporter what to write about or tell an editorial board what to opine about. They fiercely guard their independence and are quickly offended by anyone who tries to reduce their independence. Don't ever expect that they are going to let you read their story before it goes to print; it's not going to happen.

- Invitations to respond. Often an editorial board or one of the officers of the newspaper will invite a City Manager to let them know if they disagree with one of their positions. Don't ever do it; you are probably being baited. The few times, in different cities, I have tried to take issue with the position of a newspaper, I have received a thousand reasons and justifications why they are right in their opinion and I am wrong. They just wanted to argue or to gloat. My conclusion is that they are not serious about receiving contrary points of view. Trust me; they have already thought through the various points of view. The invitation is merely an opportunity for them to gloat about their intelligence and their reasoning and to gain satisfaction in knowing that they got under your skin. Don't give them the satisfaction. They own the paper; they own the ink; they own the distribution system. They will use it as they see fit.

  Factual issues are another story, so to speak. If they get a fact wrong, feel free to correct them. Just don't expect the correction to have the same prominent exposure in their newspaper as the original mistake.

- Objectivity and fairness. If you expect the media to be fair, objective and factual, you need to re-evaluate your expectations. Sometimes they are and sometimes they are not. I cannot even begin to count the times a reporter has interviewed me on a topic, and it was as if they already had their story written. They were simply trying to get me to give them the quotes about their preconceived content so they could just drop them into their already written story. In one city, the reporter didn't even interview me or another city official. They just made up their facts and their interpretation of those facts. This type of poor journalism encourages cities to disregard commercial media, establish their own information networks and provide information directly to their constituents.

- <u>Newspaper Hierarchy.</u> As much as some people want you to believe that reporters have complete independence in the stories they write, the newspaper business is very hierarchal. Editors tell reporters what stories to go after and what slant they want on the story. If it doesn't turn out the way they want, they may edit the story. They also write the headline to give the story the punch and direction they want. Publishers tell Editors what to do. Owners tell Publishers what to do. You may hear a lot of rhetoric about the free press being the guardian of democracy, etc. Be cautious how you interpret and apply that.

- <u>Staff Spies.</u> The news media cultivates its sources. Every City Manager should rest assured that the news media have sources inside of City Hall. If you think they don't, think again. It always happens. Even if it doesn't, you should act like it does.

    To me, the question isn't IF something should be released to the public because, in the public sector, it will always be released. The question is WHEN should it be released? Releasing information before the facts are fully known or before the City Council knows and acts on it can be harmful to the city. Finding the right timing can often be a challenge. Having media spies inside of your organization that give tips to reporters regarding questions they should prematurely ask can seriously mess with the timing of the release of important information. Be cautious, even inside of your own organization, about the handling of sensitive information.

This puts me in mind of a story. Although it is unrelated directly to the media, it demonstrates the reality of internal spies and is interesting and instructional to City Managers. On one occasion, some of the employees were very curious about my strategy for managing the city. I was an outsider and they simply did not know what to expect. For weeks I was suspicious that someone was visiting my office at night and looking at my papers. When I came to the office in the morning, things were not where I left them. I just became curious about who was doing it. I obtained a bottle of the purple dye that banks sometimes place on the money at teller's windows in case they are robbed. The dye attaches itself to human skin and is very hard to remove. I labeled some computer disks as "confidential," covered them in purple dye and left, as I normally did, at the end of the day. The next morning, my computer keyboard, the disk, disk box and parts of my desk were smeared with purple dye. Several of the employees called in sick and were absent for a couple of days. I expect they were busy washing and scraping their hands because, when they returned to work, there was no sign of the dye. From that time forward throughout my career, I never tried to lock my office or desk or filing cabinet. I simply assumed that people would break into my office and find access to everything. If there was ever anything confidential that I didn't want anyone to see, I kept it on my person. The same goes for verbal information. If you want to keep a secret, don't tell anyone.

- <u>City Council Involvement.</u> Every City Council I have worked with has had at least one person who shared sensitive information with the media. Some, I think, were naïve. Most, I think, were hopeful that if they shared information, they would receive favorable treatment by the media. Usually they did, for a while. In every case, the media eventually turned on them. Not to worry, however; the media always found someone else to inform them. I'm not saying this is right or ethical. I'm just saying City Managers should expect this type of thing to happen and manage it as best they can. There are some subjects, especially those discussed in executive session, that are protected by law. If Council members disclose them, they will have violated their fiduciary duty and will be subject to the penalties prescribed. I often found it helpful in those circumstances to have the City Attorney remind Council members of their duty in executive session before discussing protected information.

Radio

News programs on radio are much the same as television in that those media work with soundbites. Comments should be short and succinct, direct and to the point. For me, it always helped to pre-think the issue so that I could make an accurate comment that was quotable.

Although there can be local news programs, for the most part when we discuss radio media, we're referring to talk shows. It's interesting to me that talk shows of all sorts seem to get their material from the reports of other media, newspapers in particular. One helpful way to prepare for a talk show is to know what the newspaper is reporting. There is a good chance those topics will come up on a radio talk show. A favorite topic for local radio talk shows is what's happening at City Hall. Even though some of the dialog on these types of shows can seem crazy at times, don't underestimate the listenership and power of influence these programs have. City Managers are well advised to occasionally participate in these programs, to face the hard questions, so that the facts are kept straight and there is a counterbalance to some of the fringe comments. My experience is that the city employees are among the regular listeners of these talk shows. By occasionally appearing on them, the City Manager will be taking advantage of an opportunity to communicate with the workforce, as well.

On several occasions, I appeared on local radio talk shows. At first, I was quite hesitant to jump into a conversation. That's me in real life, not just in front of the media. After a while, I became much more comfortable with it. Although some of the dialog and many of the call-in opinions were strong, I found that the facts could be told and additional perspective added. The listenership was always broader than I expected because people would say something to me after a show about how they listened in. From my perspective, radio should not be overlooked, and City Managers should engage with it.

Television

If you manage a city that has local TV coverage, you are fortunate. Television is a powerful medium for communicating messages. The only drawback is that your message must fit inside of a 10 second, or less, window. Your sound bite must be well thought through so that it can have the punch you need to deliver your message. Keep this in mind; for interviews, live is always better than recorded. A recorded message can and will be edited to get the producers', not necessarily your, message across. For this medium, it is especially important to know your talking points and be able to express them in a very concise manner.

When I first arrived in one city, I was surprised to find that all the local TV stations had set up cameras in the gallery in the Council Chambers. It wasn't just for me on my first day on the job. It was a regular practice. I could look forward to TV interviews pretty much every week, before, during, or after City Council meetings.

A word about <u>ambush journalism</u> is in order here. This is where reporters spring an unanticipated question on you to get a negative spontaneous reaction. They are generally trying to boost viewer interest in their story. This is an underhanded journalistic technique that lacks integrity. Mostly, I have seen this technique used by stations which have lower ratings. Ratings have a huge impact on their advertising revenue. They are trying to boost their ratings by sensational reporting, generally at the city's expense. If you run across an unethical reporter, try your best to get them to play by the rules. Try talking to their boss, although don't have high expectations about that because the reporters are probably acting on direction from their superiors. Check with your Public Information Officer to get ideas about what else might be done to encourage their ethical behavior.

I recall a particularly annoying experience with a TV reporter. We had been dealing with a sensitive issue for several weeks in the City Council meeting. This reporter requested an interview "on various topics." I granted the interview on condition that he would not ask me about the sensitive topic the Council was trying to work through. I did not feel that I should say anything about it until the

Council had arrived at their decision for fear that my comments might prejudice the outcome. The reporter agreed. The interview was held in the hallway outside of the Council Chambers several minutes before the meeting was to begin. In front of the camera with the lights shining and the microphone in my face, the reporter asked several questions. I was happy to answer. Then, he suddenly pivoted on one foot to reveal a second reporter immediately behind him. She put another microphone in my face and asked the question he had agreed not to ask. I bridged the question to maintain my professional commitment to the City Council. Unfortunately, I'm sure my anger showed through. To me, the reporter's action was completely unethical and a breach of confidence, even though I'm sure the first reporter thought he was technically keeping his commitment by having someone else ask the question. I spoke to his superiors at the station, to no avail. I'm sure they sanctioned his action. Their ratings were consistently in second place and I think they were trying every strategy to boost them. For a long time, I wouldn't, couldn't really, speak to the reporter because I couldn't get his unethical behavior out of my mind, and I couldn't trust him or his station. I didn't freeze him out of the information they required; I just made sure that he got it from another source.

Internet Website

Websites and other technology were once considered by many elected officials to be "toys." Now, it's clear that they are tools, very important tools. Websites are valuable for informing the public about services and providing access to the city. Having a "virtual newsroom" allows the city to have centralized access to information through news releases, video clips and recorded meetings. Websites are also valuable as a tool for doing business such as taking electronic payments for utility service, applying for permits, or taking public input on important issues.

Every city should have a communication strategic plan. The website should be the central piece to that plan. Every other communication piece should refer people to the website for additional and more complete information.

It is possible to live-stream meetings over the internet through your website. This is a great supplement to the city's PEG (Public, Education and Government) cable TV channel, which can be used to broaden audience access.

For the most part, websites are one-way communication tools where the city provides information. They are a very, very important component in the overall strategy of engaging people.

Cable TV

Cities that have cable TV service within their borders will receive a cable franchise fee from the cable company. They will also receive complimentary access to the cable system by having a PEG (Public, Education and Government) channel assigned to them. To use the channel, technological equipment, including cameras, lighting and sound systems will be necessary. Since the franchise fee revenue is restricted in use, it can be perfectly used for this purpose. It can also be used to create studios where information pieces can be created and placed on the city's cable channel. With a PEG channel, the city can broadcast its public meetings and its information pieces to cable users. It can also make them available on the city's website and over social media. It has always surprised me how much viewership these channels get.

As I have said in previous examples, a city-operated cable TV channel is a great way to disperse information about the city. It is also a great way to encourage commercial media to be more accurate in their reporting of city issues.

Social Media

For my purposes, social media means Facebook, Twitter, and YouTube and all of their competitors. There are other forms of social media that may be useful.

A Facebook account is a great way to provide information to a constituent audience. An interested citizen would need to subscribe and become a follower of the city's account. It is an easy and popular way for people to stay current with important issues and events in the city. Meetings can be live streamed over Facebook as well as over the cable channel. We have seen people become "private reporters" for their own Facebook accounts by streaming a meeting, interviewing city officials and making comment about city issues. In today's world, any citizen can become a reporter if so wished. It was always my practice to treat citizen reporters in the same way I would a professional reporter, even though they did not have the training or the same formal commitment to journalistic ethics.

Not only can Facebook be an important source of information and engagement, but it can also be used to refer people to the city's website for more detailed information. It is not uncommon for various departments and other appendages of the city to establish their own Facebook or social media presence. I recommend that the City Manager quickly establish an executive policy on the use of social media by the municipal enterprise or it will get out of hand quickly. I have always favored a more centralized approach in such a policy so that the city's overall communication and engagement strategy can be better coordinated.

Twitter is a social medium where only relatively short written comments can be made. For city purposes, this medium is best used in the moment something is happening to refer people to the city's website to draw quick attention to a given subject. It is not best used as a central communication strategy.

Like a cable PEG channel, a YouTube channel can be created where a city can post informational video pieces about the city. Meetings can be live-streamed. They can also be recorded and posted to the YouTube channel. The advantage of the YouTube channel is that a person does not need to subscribe to a cable company to receive the information. Literally anyone in the world can log in to see the information about the city. If desired, the city can open their channel for public comments and the YouTube channel can become an even more powerful engagement tool.

Training and Professional Help

By now it should be clear that engaging the media, of all sorts, is a skill that requires time and training. It takes planning and practice to create fluid, cohesive talking points. It takes people and resources to create website and social media content. City Managers of smaller jurisdictions will need to do much of this work by themselves. City Managers of larger jurisdictions will have the benefit of hiring a professional to guide them and do much of the work. In either case, City Managers should embrace engaging the media and receive the necessary training and practice to do it well.

Engaging the Workforce

As a service industry, City government relies heavily upon its workforce to deliver services to its constituency. The better trained and informed employees are, the better they will be able to serve. It is incumbent upon City Managers to engage the workforce and treat them with extreme professionalism.

Authority is the independent right to make decisions within defined boundaries; responsibility is the obligation to make those decisions and be accountable for them. As elsewhere stated in this book, I believe the best way to manage is to delegate both authority and responsibility to the maximum possible and to the lowest reasonable level in the organization. Doing this allows and requires employees to take responsibility for their jobs, use their creativity to solve problems, and promote synergy throughout their teams. They must "own" their work. Good employees love this style of management. It will be surprising how creative they can be and how much they can get done. This style of management requires an engaged workforce and an engaging City Manager.

If engaging the workforce isn't your natural management style, here's some additional motivation for reconsidering it. In my experience, it is rare to see a City Manager lose the confidence of the City Council before first losing the confidence of the workforce. It may not be what City Managers expect, but every City Council member will have contacts inside of the city organization that they rely upon to give them the "real scoop" about what is happening on the inside. Members of the workforce will sometimes seek out a relationship with elected officials or nurture one that already existed before the Council Member was elected. To dispel the image of favoritism or insubordination, these contacts are generally secret and covert, but they exist, nonetheless. It is reality. If the City Council receives different messages from the City Manager and their contacts in the workforce, there will be problems. Be prepared for the City Council to believe their inside contacts before they believe you. Keeping the workforce informed is good practice. Listening to their concerns and ideas is good practice. Maintaining an open, honest and genuine relationship with both the workforce and the City Council is the best alternative for City Managers to pursue. Even if the City Council becomes disenchanted with their City Manager, if the workforce respects the City Manager, the City Council will approach the situation more carefully and professionally than they otherwise might have done.

Keep in mind that, "engaging" involves both informing and listening. Neither of those alone will achieve the optimal result. In addition to the application of standard interpersonal skills, here are some structured ways I have found helpful in engaging the workforce:

Team Meetings

There are many occasions to pull teams together to work on projects. These teams are an excellent opportunity for the City Manager to interact one-on-one with the people working on them. This interaction gives the City Manager the opportunity to get to know people and their capabilities better. It also gives the team members the opportunity to get to know the City Manager better. In this environment there will be occasion to exchange ideas, explore alternatives and generally engage with each other.

> Safety Training. Especially in the public works departments, periodic training meetings are held to promote personal and vehicle safety. These are also great opportunities for the City Manager to occasionally join. While there the City Manager can inform that part of the workforce about current issues in the City and address any questions they may have. I have found this form of engagement to be very effective and helpful.
>
> Shift Changes. When shifts are changing in public safety and public works departments, there is generally some sort of combined shift briefing that takes place so that the shift coming on can get acquainted with the issues that the retiring shift has been handling. These shift change briefings are a great time for the City Manager to catch and engage shift work employees that are otherwise difficult to reach. Information and engagements need to be well thought out and brief so that the work is not unreasonably interfered with and so that their time can be respected.

Briefings

Many different types of briefings are required to manage a city well. Each one is an opportunity to engage with other people. The following are several types of briefings that are common and that I have successfully used in the cities I have managed:

Status Reports and Informational Briefings. I find, especially when I'm new on a job, that I need to learn about many things that are happening. Getting status reports from staff members who've been working on the issue is a great way to come up to speed on the issues and it is a great way to get to know the staff members. The questions and answers that naturally flow from such a meeting are the heart of engagement.

New Employee Orientations. Many cities have an on-boarding process for new employees that includes briefings from various departments and orientation to city policy and issues. These are great opportunities to inform and engage people who are brand new to the organization. Oftentimes their exposure to the city is limited so their questions may be shallow, but occasionally they will surprise you. City Managers can learn a lot from these new recruits, and they can set a tone for future engagement that will pay dividends.

Video Briefings and the Use of Technology. Any briefing, be it to senior staff or a small group of the workforce, can be videotaped and presented as a training video to the members of the workforce who were not present. The videos could be posted to the website, intranet or YouTube channel for employees to watch at their leisure. The disadvantage, of course, is that watching the briefing after the fact does not allow for the same level of engagement, even if the video-taped group asked all the pertinent questions. It is more informational at that point rather than engaging. I personally prefer face-to-face meetings with employees, but, if your city is large or spread out, or for other reasons a physical gathering is not possible, you may organize virtual meetings through technology. Presentations can be made, and real-time questions and answers can be accomplished, even at remote locations throughout the city.

Newsletters

Even though it is difficult to keep information contained in newsletters current and applicable, they have always been popular with a segment of the workforce. Newsletters are more informational in nature where any questions suggestions or interaction come well after the printing and distribution.

A popular variation on the traditional newsletter is an electronic newsletter. It has the same form and same idea; it's just digital rather than printed. It can be emailed to employees or posted to the city's intranet. For those few employees who do not have regular email access, it can be printed and posted to a departmental bulletin board.

Community newsletters can be handled in similar ways as employee newsletters.

Intranet

Unlike the internet, which is open to the entire world, an intranet is a closed system which is only available to city employees. Information such as newsletters, policies, videos and information that pertains only to the workforce can be posted to this system.

Surveys

Occasionally it is helpful to conduct a survey of the workforce to find out what issues are affecting them and what could help them in their jobs. Surveys should be statistically valid, unbiased and anonymous. When beginning a survey, the City Manager should have the end purpose in mind and should know what is going to be done with the survey information once it is received, and, of course, be committed to using the data in a constructive way. Another important concept is that surveys should be kept consistent from year to year so that meaningful comparisons can be made.

Focus Groups

A Focus Group is a small group of stakeholders who meet with a facilitator to ask and answer questions about a specific topic. After a survey has been completed, data collected and conclusions drawn, Focus Groups can be held to validate the information or get greater detail regarding it. Focus Groups help to better understand and apply the information gained. They burrow into another level of detail beyond the survey, and they make the surveys more engaging.

Caution

City Managers must be very careful to be impartial and fair in all they do with the City Council, the public and with the City's workforce. I recommend against establishing personal friendships with any of these that could be interpreted as favoritism. In my view, keeping an arm's length while always being congenial and professional is best.

I recall a specific instance where a community activist reached out, wanting to become friends. As I kept her at arm's length, she then reached out to my wife. Being new in town, it would have been good for my wife to have local friends, but knowing the problems that could cause for me, I discouraged it. The friendship developed anyway. It ended poorly when it became crystal clear that the ultimate motive for the friendship was to influence me in my city work. In the same way that City Managers should be politically aware without being political, they should be friendly without having close friends attached to their city duties.

In Summary, How to Engage People

In this final chapter we have considered the fourth duty of a City Manager, Engaging People. Engaging involves informing, listening, and involving people in the business of the city. There are four distinct groups that require the attention of the engaging City Manager: the community at large, other governments, the media, and the city's workforce. This chapter has given specifics on how to engage each of these groups. The last thought regarding engagement is that it is not only the duty of the City Manager but of the entire city organization. The City Manager must ensure that it is part of the management culture.

CONCLUSION

Conclusion

Cities are of ancient origin and those who know about these things speculate that people gathered in cities to promote trade, provide mutual protection, develop specialization and do other things together that they could not do individually. Those same purposes are served by cities today. In the United States, there are many thousands of cities, ranging in size and complexity.

Modern cities may be governed in several ways. One of the most popular and effective ways is by use of the Council-Manager form of government which provides for a professional City Manager as a key part of the governance and management structure of the city. While it is true that a City Council could appoint virtually anyone to be the City Manager, the Council-Manager plan works best when the City Manager knows what cities do, how they work, and how to manage a complex municipal organization.

My graduate school internship and my first job were in a city whose City Manager had been appointed by the Mayor, his childhood best friend. The City Manager had no prior municipal experience. He was effective in his job until the city began to grow exponentially. The state of affairs began to be overwhelming and conditions became extraordinarily challenging. After a lot of difficulty and heartbreaking conflict, the City Council adopted a Council-Manager governance ordinance and brought in a manager who had been schooled in the profession. The challenges, of course, remained but the growing pains were being addressed. The city stayed committed to the concept of having professional appointed leadership, which has been a benefit to them ever since. I suspect that specific city's experience is not a lot different than many other cities throughout the nation.

The first appointment of an individual to a position like that of today's local government manager occurred in 1908 in Staunton, Virginia, where a "general manager" was employed to oversee the administrative functions of the municipality. The first formal adoption of the Council-Manager plan took place in Sumter, South Carolina, in

1912. The following year, Westmount, Quebec, adopted the plan and so introduced the Council-Manager form of government to Canada. In 1914, Dayton, Ohio, accepted the Council-Manager plan and became the first municipality of substantial size to operate under the new form of government. Sixteen years later, Durham County, North Carolina, became the first county to institute a form of government that embodied the concept of professional management.[7]

The Council-Manager plan and the city management profession were born out of the good government movement in the United States in the early 1900's. The intent of that movement was to take corruption out of city government and replace it with efficiency and fairness. City Managers continue to play a key role in accomplishing those goals even today. That is why ethics and expertise are of critical importance. As they do their work, City Managers have four primary duties to perform. The better they do these four things, the better will be the quality of life in their communities. Those four duties include:

1. Providing Leadership
2. Advising the City Council
3. Managing City Operations and
4. Engaging People.

Being a City Manager is not a casual profession; it is not for the faint hearted. The challenges are huge and growing with the complexities of our society. Those who take on the challenge must have high levels of expertise and they need to be committed to more than putting in their time and collecting their paycheck. They must model the high ideals of public service and need to be willing to persevere the rigors of issues, events and people that can sometimes be bone crushingly difficult.

Within a few short months of my first appointment as City Manager, I began feeling pressure in my chest. I was still a young

---

[7] See ICMA.org, ICMA History. Used by permission.

man but, since there was a strong history of it in my family, I thought I was having heart trouble. I went to a medical specialist and had a full cardiac examination. Following the exam and after the results of all the testing had been received, I went back in for a debriefing from the doctor. He sat me down and looked me in the eye. I was prepared for the worst. He said, "Young man, you have stress." I couldn't believe what I was hearing. There was no way, I thought, that what I was feeling physically could be due to stress. There had to be something else wrong. After all, I had been serving in the city for several years before being appointed as City Manager and I hadn't felt this kind of stress. I was in denial for about two weeks. After I finally accepted the doctor's prognosis, I changed my diet, exercise program, and way of thinking about issues at work. I learned to detect the signs of stress and manage them. I maintained those new habits throughout the course of my career. That was my first introduction to the rigors of city management.

Additionally, anyone wishing to enter the profession should understand that being a City Manager will not make you wealthy. If being wealthy is your goal, you should further explore employment in the private sector. You can earn a good living as a City Manager, but, if you get wealthy doing it, you should probably be in jail. It is a position of high public trust. For those willing to take on the challenges, I can think of no greater reward than the satisfaction of doing a job that blesses the lives of so many people.

Ingram Content Group UK Ltd.
Milton Keynes UK
UKHW021948150623
423516UK00013B/508